D1269183

CONDUCTING SCIENCE-BASED PSYCHOLOGY RESEARCH IN SCHOOLS

CONDUCTING SCIENCE-BASED PSYCHOLOGY RESEARCH IN SCHOOLS

EDITED BY

LISA M. DINELLA

AMERICAN PSYCHOLOGICAL ASSOCIATION
WASHINGTON, DC

Published by
American Psychological Association
750 First Street, NE
Washington, DC 20002
www.apa.org

To order
APA Order Department
P.O. Box 92984
Washington, DC 20090-2984
Tel: (800) 374-2721; Direct: (202) 336-5510
Fax: (202) 336-5502; TDD/TTY: (202) 336-6123
Online: www.apa.org/books/
E-mail: order@apa.org

In the U.K., Europe, Africa, and the Middle East, copies may be ordered from
American Psychological Association
3 Henrietta Street
Covent Garden, London
WC2E 8LU England

Typeset in Minion by Circle Graphics, Columbia, MD

Printer: Maple-Vail, Binghamton, NY
Cover Designer: Berg Design, Albany, NY
Technical/Production Editor: Kathryn Funk

The opinions and statements published are the responsibility of the authors, and such opinions and statements do not necessarily represent the policies of the American Psychological Association.

Library of Congress Cataloging-in-Publication Data

Conducting science-based psychology research in schools / edited by Lisa M. Dinella. — 1st ed.
    p. cm.
  ISBN-13: 978-1-4338-0468-7
  ISBN-10: 1-4338-0468-9
  1. Psychology—Research. 2. Educational psychology—Research. I. Dinella, Lisa M.

  BF76.5.C64 2009
  150.72—dc22
                        2008049772

British Library Cataloguing-in-Publication Data
A CIP record is available from the British Library.

Printed in the United States of America
First Edition

June 24, 2009

I would like to dedicate this book to the school professionals who devote their lives to educating students. I especially would like to recognize my mother, Diana Dinella, who has been an elementary school teacher for over 30 years. This book is proof that mothers know best, as she predicted when I was in elementary school that I would be either a teacher or an editor—and now I am both.

Contents

Contributors

J. Lawrence Aber, New York University, New York City

Amy Bellmore, University of Wisconsin—Madison

Joshua L. Brown, Fordham University, Bronx, NY

Elise Cappella, New York University, New York City

Lia Chomat-Mooney, University of Virginia, Charlottesville

Jennifer Coyne Cassata, Prince William County Public Schools, Manassas, VA

Lisa M. Dinella, Monmouth University, West Long Branch, NJ

Celene E. Domitrovich, The Pennsylvania State University, University Park

Gwen A. Frishkoff, University of Pittsburgh, Pittsburgh, PA

Gary Gottfredson, University of Maryland, College Park

Sandra Graham, University of California, Los Angeles

Mark T. Greenberg, The Pennsylvania State University, University Park

Bridget K. Hamre, University of Virginia, Charlottesville

Stephanie M. Jones, Harvard University, Cambridge, MA

Gary Ladd, Arizona State University, Tempe

Maria D. LaRusso, New York University, New York City, and Universidad de Los Andes, Bogatá, Colombia

Greta M. Massetti, University at Buffalo, State University of New York

Charles A. Perfetti, University of Pittsburgh, Pittsburgh, PA

Robert C. Pianta, University of Virginia, Charlottesville

Sylvia Rosenfield, University of Maryland, College Park

Amy Silverman, University of Maryland, College Park

Mari Strand Cary, Carnegie Mellon University, Pittsburgh, PA

Heather K. Warren, George Mason University, Fairfax, VA

Gregory White, National Academy of Education, Washington, DC

Sasha Yampolsky, Tufts University, Medford, MA, and Massachusetts General Hospital, Boston

Foreword:
Insights From Young Scholars
on the Frontier
Between Psychological
and Education Sciences

In the fall of 2003, 13 talented psychology PhDs were invited to become postdoctoral fellows in a unique program designed to attract psychological scientists to conduct research at the interface of psychology and education. The Institute of Education Sciences awarded the American Psychological Association funding to create this pilot program with the idea that it would harness psychology's science of learning and bio-psychosocial models to the rigorous methodological training experienced in graduate psychology and apply them to the education sciences.

Those of us at the American Psychological Association who helped to design the Psychology Education Research Training (PERT) program—Cynthia Belar, Gregory White, Jeanine Cogan, and I—hoped that the fellows would be successful at developing education and training models to advance school-based scientific research and increase the visibility of education research within the discipline of psychology. Most of all, the program aspired to increase the application of cutting-edge psychological science to high-quality, school-based education research.

An experimental matching program modeled after medical school residency programs was used to identify PERT fellows. Pairs of potential fellows and mentors then submitted training plans designed to show how the postdoctoral experience would prepare fellows for leadership positions in academic research. The research training plans addressed issues such as interventions for students with learning and behavioral problems, reading development, scientific reasoning skills, peer relations and psychosocial adjustment, early childhood, and teacher quality, among others. As the reader can see from this volume—one that was created, edited, and primarily written by PERT fellows—PERT program aspirations were met.

Each of the former PERT fellows featured in various chapters of this volume can be labeled as an experienced school-based researcher and can offer high-quality scholarly and practical advice to readers seeking wisdom on how to operate in the complex and demanding environment of schools. They acquired this experience by dint of their deep intelligence and intense commitment to scholarship and to improving schools. They took every opportunity to learn and grow during the fellowship and beyond.

The insights presented in this book are tested, current, and couched in psychological science. The authors provide practical information and advice to those embarking into the endlessly frustrating and fascinating world of education research. In each chapter, one can find not only a delineation of problems one will encounter but also ways to capitalize on the qualities that make schools such interesting places. There is no more important venue than schools for the most creative and well-prepared scholars interested in the future of our nation. And no more creative and well-prepared group of young scholars are better able to guide our way than the authors of this wonderful volume.

Rena F. Subotnik
Director, Center for Psychology in Schools and Education
Education Directorate
American Psychological Association

Foreword:
Meeting Future Training
Needs in School-Based
Education Research

In 2002, two pieces of legislation were enacted that are likely to have an indelible impact on education in the United States. The first, the No Child Left Behind Act (NCLB), ushered in a new era of accountability in American schools, using phrases such as "programs and practices which have been proven effective through rigorous scientific research" and "scientifically based instruction." The second, the Education Sciences Reform Act, reorganized the existing U.S. Department of Education research and evaluation units into a new entity, the Institute of Education Sciences (IES), which was designed to provide rigorous evidence to guide and support education practice and policy. These pieces of legislation were designed to work in tandem to address the information needs of policymakers, administrators, and teachers and to provide a meaningful voice for researchers conducting relevant studies in this field.

Once these policy changes were implemented, it became clear that there was a mismatch between the types of education research and evaluation work that were needed to fulfill the vision of NCLB and the existing scientific workforce. Historically, the Department of Education had not made a significant investment in training education researchers. Although the National Institutes of Health (NIH) and the National Science Foundation (NSF) had been funding education-related research conducted in schools, their training programs were not specifically designed to produce young investigators with the skill set necessary to conduct methodologically rigorous research in school-based settings. As is evidenced by the topics covered in this book, there are a host of issues specific to research in educational settings that can easily ruin the best-laid plans of a naïve researcher. Systematic and rigorous training on how to conduct research in school-based settings was needed to prepare a new cadre of education researchers.

Recognizing the need to promote the training of young scholars interested in pursuing careers in education research, Grover J. (Russ) Whitehurst, the first director of IES, awarded a grant to the American Psychological Association (APA) to support the establishment of a Psychology Education Research Training (PERT) program designed to train psychology postdoctoral fellows committed to conducting research in school-based settings. While working at IES, I had the honor of serving as the program officer for this grant, and the pleasure of meeting with the fellows on several occasions. This group of dedicated fellows, and the senior researchers who agreed to mentor them, exemplify the skills and abilities necessary to conduct high-quality education research that is relevant at both the policy and practice level. When the idea for this book surfaced, I saw it as the perfect opportunity not only to showcase the talents of these promising scholars but also to codify what they have learned about what it takes to form lasting partnerships and conduct rigorous research in school-based settings. The results speak for themselves.

The APA PERT program was a success, and IES decided to expand the scope and breadth of training available by creating a Predoctoral Interdisciplinary Research Training grant program in 2004 and a Postdoctoral Interdisciplinary Research Training grant program in 2005; I also served as the first program officer for these training grants. These training grants provide institutional support for programs that train scholars from disciplines such as psychology, education, sociology, economics, demography, and neuroscience on the theory, methods, and logistics of conducting research in school-based settings. Information on these training programs can be found at http://ies.ed.gov/ncer/projects/. Feedback from both faculty and fellows suggests that these grants have supported the creation of programs that cut across disciplinary lines and provide research training opportunities that would not otherwise exist. Coupled with the ongoing fellowship programs supported by NIH and NSF, and the training that takes place as part of the research grants funded by all three agencies, there is now a much greater capacity to meet the training needs of the field. Of course, the true measure of the success of all these training efforts is the growing number of talented education researchers who are conducting studies that will inform our policies and practices and ultimately improve the educational attainment and well-being of our children. This book makes an important contribution toward that goal.

James A. Griffin
Deputy Chief
Child Development and Behavior Branch
Eunice Kennedy Shriver National Institute of Child Health
and Human Development
National Institutes of Health
U.S. Department of Health and Human Services

Acknowledgments

The authors would like to acknowledge and thank the American Psychological Association and the Institute of Education Sciences for the opportunity to be a part of the Postdoctoral Education Research Training program. The program served as an invaluable professional development forum, strengthening a network of professionals dedicated to the advancement of psychology research within school-based settings. This book is just one of the many products of the program.

Conducting Science-Based Psychology Research in Schools

Introduction

Lisa M. Dinella

The primary goal of this book is to provide those interested in conducting quality psychological research in a school-based setting with an informed framework for starting and maintaining such a research program, thus addressing the field's need for guidelines on conducting research in school settings. The book is different from traditional experimental design texts in that it goes beyond reviewing methodological and measurement issues to counsel researchers on how to avoid the common pitfalls experienced by those new to conducting psychological research in schools. The authors walk investigators through the research process from beginning to end, providing practical strategies and pragmatic advice on how to conduct high quality empirical research in a school-based setting. Further, chapters are highlighted by the insights of education professionals with whom the authors collaborate.

The book is built on two key premises. First, quality scientific research is necessary to forward education and to best serve students, families, and education professionals. This book discusses how to apply scientific principles and methods to the reality of school settings. Second, scientific research is not quality research without the collaboration of school stakeholders. The authors present a novel framework for conducting psychological research *with* schools rather than *on* or *in* schools. The importance of the relationship built between researcher and educational professional is emphasized in the framework of the text; in that input from the education professionals in the authors' schools are included throughout the book.

THEORETICAL AND EMPIRICAL BASIS
FOR THE BOOK

As evidenced by the diversity of our authors' research programs, the theoretical backgrounds driving our individual research programs are varied. However, there are some overarching perspectives that drive our collaboration.

- Scientific information is necessary to inform psychologists, educational professionals, and decision makers about how to improve the educational system for the well-being of all students.
- Interdisciplinary approaches are necessary for bridging the scientific processes commonly used in the domains of psychology and education. This infrastructure could be applied to a variety of disciplines in terms of their relationship with education.
- Schools are a natural context in which to study young people and by extension the important individuals and systems that influence young people's lives. Therefore, both educational and psychological issues can and should be examined within the school realm.
- Schools are also a natural context in which to research, design, test, apply, and improve interventions.
- Lastly, and maybe most important, psychologists need to better understand how to work *with* schools and educational researchers, school professionals, students, and families. And, it is paramount for researchers to remember that although schools are a wonderful resource for learning about educational and psychological issues, the main goal within a school is the education of the students. Researchers are also responsible for informing education professionals on how to take advantage of the scientific processes used daily by psychologists and how to incorporate relevant findings into their practice.

FITTING OUR APPROACH INTO CONTEMPORARY
THEORY, RESEARCH, AND APPLICATION

The call for quality research in school environments has been made, and recently guidelines have been set forth for promoting and furthering sound empirical study. Our work forwards the call for rigorous research standards by providing psychological researchers with practical guidelines on how to design and implement said research.

A cornerstone of our work is the National Research Council's report *Scientific Research in Education* (Shavelson & Towne, 2002) that calls for rigorous empirical research to be conducted in school settings and defines quality work. In addition, we embrace the 12 recommendations made by Towne and colleagues in *Advancing Scientific Research in Education* (Towne, Wise, & Winters, 2004) detailing how the field should best promote school-based research. However, more information is needed about implementing psychological research that marries rigor with relevance in school settings. This book addresses the field's need for a set of guidelines outlining the pragmatics of conducting psychological research in the complex setting of our education system.

ORGANIZATIONAL STRUCTURE OF THE BOOK

The structure of the book parallels the natural progression of the research process, beginning with information about initiating and maintaining relationships with school stakeholders, followed by recommendations about research design and methodology, and finally concluding with guidance about disseminating research findings. Each chapter also incorporates the viewpoints of the school professionals with whom the authors partner. The following provides a brief overview of each chapter.

In chapter 1, Lisa M. Dinella and Gary Ladd share their approaches and techniques to building and maintaining successful relationships with all school stakeholders, especially the school administration, teachers, parents, and students. Each researcher who enters a school inevitably leaves a legacy—and the intent of this chapter is to help researchers build a legacy that they can be proud of, that serves their community well, and that paves the way for future research collaborations. Interviews with prominent school stakeholders from one longitudinal research project are included to elucidate relationship building from multiple perspectives.

School-based researchers will find it easier to coordinate college and university Institutional Review Board (IRB) processes with those at the school level if they fully understand those processes, anticipate obstacles, and work with, rather than against, the cultures of potential partner schools. Thus, in chapter 2, Mari Strand Cary addresses the purpose and requirements of IRBs (including the unique challenge school-based research poses to university IRBs), provides general strategies for researchers to use as they seek to establish partnerships with schools, and describes oft-held views schools hold regarding research and study approval processes.

In chapter 3, Elise Cappella, Greta M. Massetti, and Sasha Yampolsky provide an overview of the promises and potential pitfalls of randomization in school-based intervention studies, including practical guidelines regarding when, where, and how to use a randomized design. The overall aim is to guide school-based intervention researchers to design meaningful studies that balance the central goals of community responsiveness and methodological rigor.

Chapter 4, by Bridget K. Hamre, Robert C. Pianta, and Lia Chomat-Mooney, focuses on ways researchers can use observational methods to inform important questions in school-based research. The chapter begins with a brief introduction to the history of classroom observation and then provides a theory on classrooms that gives guidance to researchers deciding which aspects of classrooms are most important to observe. The authors then discuss issues related to designing observational methodology. They provide information on the logistics of conducting classroom observations, addressing common areas of concern, such as how long and when to observe to obtain a representative sample of the classroom environment. In the last section, the authors discuss current limitations in classroom observation research and suggest several areas for future research and measure development.

Chapter 5, by Amy Silverman, Jennifer Coyne Cassata, Gary Gottfredson, and Sylvia Rosenfield, serves as a practical guide to help researchers navigate the complex processes of choosing and developing measures for use in school-based research. The authors highlight the scientific and practical considerations that researchers and school representatives should think about before deciding whether to use existing measures, whether to adapt measures that currently exist in the scientific literature or school community, or whether to develop new measures. As part of discussing this process, the chapter considers the types of measures available to researchers conducting research in schools.

Chapter 6, an interdisciplinary chapter by Heather K. Warren, Celene E. Domitrovich, and Mark T. Greenberg, highlights the theoretical contribution of a conceptual model of implementation quality for school-based programming from the field of prevention science and informed by community perspectives. The authors introduce a broad conceptual model of implementation for school-based programs to serve as a practical guide for understanding the critical dimensions of implementation quality that should be monitored while utilizing empirically based interventions. The implications of these issues for researchers involved in delivering programs within schools are also considered to assist contemporary scientists in various roles establish collaborative interactions with schools.

The study of learning is a core research area in psychology, and results in this field may have important implications for evidence-based research and practice in schools. In chapter 7, Gwen A. Frishkoff, Gregory White, and Charles A. Perfetti focus on recent evidence that supports the need for more translational research, which they characterize as research that (a) is conducted in vivo (in real learning environments, i.e., classrooms) and (b) involves active collaborations between researchers trained in cognitive, learning, and developmental sciences and educational researchers and practitioners. Furthermore, the chapter provides information on the use of school-based technologies and cognitively based interventions. The chapter concludes with an outline of challenges in the development and implementation of methods to support translational research in schools.

School context is a factor that must be considered in the design and implementation of any school-based study. Thus, the goals of chapter 8, by Maria D. LaRusso, Joshua L. Brown, Stephanie M. Jones, and J. Lawrence Aber, are to highlight the complexity and importance of school contexts, to provide an overview of the many ways in which one can assess and analyze school contexts, and to describe a number of practical issues in conducting research in and on school contexts.

For evidence-based research to be translated into evidence-based practice, researchers are challenged to disseminate their research results beyond the walls of academia and into both professional and lay communities. Adopting broad dissemination as a goal is especially important for school-based research given the large number of stakeholders who stand to benefit from rigorous educational research. The main goals of chapter 9, by Amy Bellmore and Sandra Graham, are to examine whether findings from school-based research are currently reaching diverse audiences and to discuss effective outlets for reaching audiences.

REFERENCES

Shavelson, R. J., & Towne, L. (Eds.). (2002). *Scientific research in education.* Washington, DC: National Research Council, National Academies Press.
Towne, L., Wise, L. L., & Winters, T. M. (Eds.). (2004). *Advancing scientific research in education.* Washington, DC: National Research Council, National Academies Press.

1

Building and Maintaining Relationships With School Stakeholders

Lisa M. Dinella and Gary Ladd

This book is based on the premise that school-based research, for all who participate, is enhanced when investigators collaborate with school personnel or stakeholders. Throughout our combined years of experience with multiple school-based research programs, we have found that collaborative and reciprocal relationships between research teams and school stakeholders enhance the process, quality, and outcomes of school-based investigations. In this chapter, we consider some of the approaches and techniques that we have found useful for building and maintaining successful relationships with school administrators, teachers, students, and families. In particular, we illustrate approaches to relationship building that were developed as part of the Pathways Project, a 15-year prospective longitudinal study of students' academic and psychological development (see Ladd, 2005).

BUILDING A PARTNERSHIP VERSUS RECRUITING A SAMPLE

Most researchers are taught to address their questions by relying on theory, constructing testable models, generating specific hypotheses, and identifying appropriate samples, measures (e.g., observations, surveys, interviews), and data-analytic techniques. Often what is lacking in researchers' education, however, is instruction on how to translate a well-designed proposal into a rigorous and fully operational investigation within real-world contexts such as schools. This can be achieved, we contend, by encouraging investigators to learn about schools, schooling, and issues that are central to partnerships with school personnel. Particularly important is knowledge about the culture, organization, and administration of schools; the roles and responsibilities of school personnel (the stakeholders); and the processes that occur in classrooms (i.e., schooling). Achieving this kind of perspective has the potential to enhance educational research.

A common way for investigators to conduct research is to identify a set of research objectives and then search out and recruit a sample that can be used to test their hypotheses. Often, sample selection and recruitment procedures are guided by efficiencies such as time constraints, ease of access to participants, and cost-effectiveness. Moreover, sometimes these efficiencies come at a cost (e.g., limits imposed on research procedures, reduced sample participation, attrition, poor sample representativeness or generalizability[1]).

As an alternative, we challenge school-based researchers to shift their perspective from one of gaining access to participants and recruitment of a sample to one that emphasizes building a partnership with school stakeholders. This raises the question of why it is important to build relationships with a wide array of school stakeholders, even if an investigator is primarily interested in the feedback of a select group of participants within a school, such as students or teachers. Our experiences suggest that full collaboration between schools and researchers leads to an environment that benefits both the school and the research team, both immediately and over time. Open communication and mutual agreement on goals often benefit all partners.

Fundamental areas for discussion include defining the scope of a research program, devising an investigative timeline, identifying scheduling conflicts or problems, devising research questions that are of interest to all parties, minimizing the obtrusiveness of data collection procedures, and sharing researchers' and schools' resources. Benefits that may accrue as a result of well-established partnerships will be considered in greater

---

[1] See chapter 2, this volume, for a discussion on how many Institutional Review Board processes reinforce a researcher-centered focus rather than a collaborative focus.

detail throughout this chapter. In the sections that follow, we identify some of the major stakeholders in schools and consider the importance of relationship building.

IDENTIFYING STAKEHOLDERS AND BUILDING PARTNERSHIPS

Collaborative relationships benefit both school personnel and researchers because they have the potential to enhance the scope, quality, and applicability of the findings that are obtained from educational research. For school-based researchers, the process of building these partnerships begins with knowing who the primary stakeholders are within a school and understanding their contribution to the school environment. Within a school, it can be beneficial to establish relationships with individuals across many areas of the school or create a network of partnerships.

To establish such a network, an important first step for researchers is to learn as much as possible about the culture of the school systems they wish to approach. Each school system has its own culture and organization. For example, variables such as the size and socioeconomic status of the student body and the level of community involvement (e.g., parents, taxpayers) contribute to a school's individuality. Furthermore, schools differ on dimensions such as sponsorships, philosophies, and missions (e.g., private, single-sex, religious, charter), which in turn shape their cultures and organizational structures.

As an illustration, the typical organizational structure for a medium-sized school district (20,000 students) is shown in Figure 1.1. The complexity of the elements within this figure helps one appreciate the size of the task that school personnel confront on a daily basis. Researchers who enter this web must work in unison with school personnel and try not to disrupt a school's working balance. Furthermore, researchers must recognize that school personnel have, as their primary duty, the responsibility of maintaining this balance (for students' sakes). Thus, when school personnel express hesitations about admitting research programs into their schools, it may be because they have concerns about how a project might affect their school's functioning and balance.

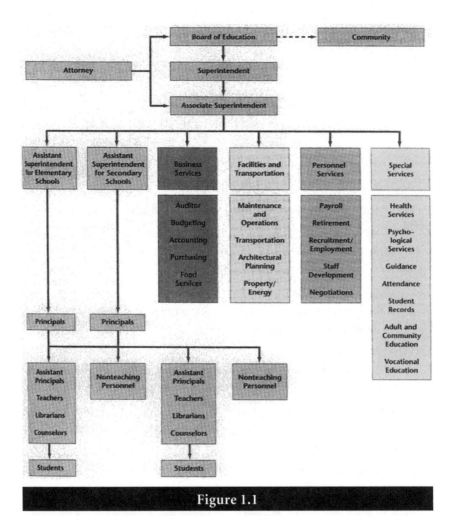

Figure 1.1

Organizational structure of a typical school district. From *Becoming A Teacher,* 4th ed. (p. 171), by F. W. Parkay and B. H. Stanford, 1998, Boston: Allyn & Bacon. Copyright 1998 by Pearson Education. Reprinted with permission of the publisher.

Although each school is unique, there are some commonalities in the personnel who work in schools. Thus, it is instructive to identify the primary employees within the school setting, consider their basic job descriptions or duties, and reflect on why it is important to establish partnerships with these persons. Figure 1.1 illustrates many of the primary employees that researchers should be considering when designing and implementing a school-based research project, and how these employee positions relate to one another. Next, we consider six categories of school personnel and some of the benefits that researchers may derive from partnering with each. We also consider the typical priorities of each individual and offer tips for researchers on how to form working relationships.

Superintendents and Board of Education

School superintendents ensure that their districts operate within federal, state, and local regulations. Included among the superintendents' responsibilities are overseeing the hiring of personnel, acting as a liaison between the schools and the community, and recommending educational programs for adoption within the school district. The superintendent and school board usually collaborate closely on any major changes that occur within the district.

The board of education, or school board, is composed of anywhere from 5 to 15 community members who are elected as a governing board for a school district (see Parkay & Stanford, 1998, for a review). Members of a school board are usually paid and serve a minimum term of about 4 years. Included among their responsibilities are approving personnel hires conducted by superintendents, creating governing policies for the school district, and overseeing performance assessments of curriculum and personnel. School boards are designed to provide the community with a voice in the functioning of local schools, not only by having their membership composed of community members but also by allowing time for the input of any community member who attends regularly scheduled school board meetings. The level of input and control school boards have within their schools varies, as does their interaction with the superintendent of schools.

Why Meet With the Superintendent and School Board?

Most often, investigators meet with superintendents and board members when they are initiating a research partnership. Researchers may attend school board meetings to present their research program and goals and to propose the formation of a partnership. If interest in partnership is garnered at this level, researchers can then begin discussions with school principals. In some school districts, the board and/or superintendent serve as the district's institutional review board (IRB), and researchers are required to gain their approval prior to beginning any research. Some large school districts or those located near large research universities have their own stand-alone IRB, headed by research and evaluation directors. It is often necessary for research to be approved at this level before it can be discussed with a school board or superintendent. Researchers may find that partnerships form more smoothly and effectively when they understand the school district's procedures for obtaining permission before they contact schools and before they make formal presentations or requests to conduct research. Building a rapport with research and evaluation directors can be beneficial to this end (see chap. 2, this volume, for more information about IRBs, research and evaluation directors, and approval processes). Regardless of whether IRB or other forms of approval are required, investigators who wish to propose large-scale or high-profile research programs may choose to meet with school superintendents and board members.

Designing a Presentation for the Superintendent and School Board

Presenting the goals of a research program to the superintendent and school board can be viewed as an early opportunity for researchers to forge a productive partnership with schools. Several strategies may help researchers achieve this end. First, during initial meetings, researchers should describe their project (recognizing the possibility of collaborative modifications) and enumerate its potential benefits to science as well as to schools, children, and community members as succinctly and accurately as possible. Care should be taken to explore the potential costs and benefits of the proposed partnership, as well as the methods and procedures that will be used to answer the project's questions. Furthermore, researchers should be clear on how the results of the study will be disseminated and the timeline and method for making the results available to the school. These steps will allow board members and superintendents to understand the parameters of the requested partnership.

When presenting this information, researchers should keep in mind that their audience is highly skilled as well as highly educated and informed about topics related to education. However, presentations that are laden with rhetoric or scientific jargon may prevent school personnel from understanding the research program and its importance and run the risk of making researchers and their projects seem inaccessible. Researchers will be well served by striking a balance between informing administrators and overwhelming them with information.

Researchers may also want to consider the benefits and costs of their research program from the perspective of a school board or superintendent before they meet with these personnel. Doing so may better prepare them to answer questions about the proposed partnership. School boards and superintendents have the responsibility of asking, "How will this program benefit the students and the school community?" and "How will the community view this partnership?" Presentations that address these questions directly may anticipate administrators' concerns, address some of the hidden barriers that often interfere with partnership formation, and make the decision process easier for school personnel. Moreover, partnerships established this way lay the foundation for a relationship built on open communication.

Principals

In most districts, principals are the chief administrators of individual schools. Principals are usually the most visible and accessible figure associated with the school because they serve to connect all of the employees and staff members within their school to the upper levels of administration and to their community. The principals' primary responsibility is the leadership of their school's teachers; however, their job responsibilities are extensive and include (a) educational leadership within their school, (b) facilitating communication between all school members, (c) school and community relations, (d) interaction with students, and (e) management issues (National Association of Elementary School Principals, 2001). Researchers who build reciprocal relations with school principals open the door to the creation of joint goals between schools and researchers.

Working With Principals

It is common for researchers to work closely with principals during the initial stages of their research program. This early relationship can be particularly beneficial for addressing many of the logistical hurdles that arise when investigators attempt to integrate research procedures into school environments. Researchers can propose a research process, and principals can advise them about how best to apply their methodologies within the culture and environment of their particular school. In these conversations with principals, researchers may find it helpful to present the planned methodology as a "wish list," communicating to principals that their original plan can be adjusted to meet the needs of the school. Changes that might adversely affect the design of the research or seriously alter the researchers' goals can be problem solved. Working together, principals and researchers can partner to devise a strategy that takes both the needs of the school and the research project into consideration, thus addressing the needs of the school and requirements that ensure "good science." A respectful relationship between principals and the research scientists can promote creativity and compromises that maximize both parties' goals.

In addition to conversations about research objectives and requirements, early discussions with principals can help researchers negotiate a schedule for data collection that balances constraints inherent within schools and the timeline of the research project. Topics discussed may include holidays and school events and working around standardized testing schedules. Principals can help researchers reach program milestones and timelines by identifying the best sources of reliable data, such as teachers who are likely to be willing participants. Finally, but potentially most important, this relationship can open discourse that ensures that both parties understand and commit to a level of investment (e.g., in time, resources) that is necessary for a project to succeed. Miscommunications about time investments can cause school personnel to feel overwhelmed and undervalued, which in turn can lead to poor data quality and in some cases premature termination of a project and partnership. Open and honest discussions can prevent these outcomes.

Principals also have the ability to act as a liaison between the research program and the teachers, students, and parents within a school, and they can coordinate other employees, such as the support staff. By serving as a project's liaison, principals can increase a school's investment or "buy-in" in the research program. When the members of a school are invested in a research program, the responsibility for success becomes a shared venture. Principals can increase buy-in in three ways: (a) by showing enthusiasm for the project with other school stakeholders, (b) by helping researchers frame arguments for their project in ways that are sensitive to the needs of various subgroups of school stakeholders, and (c) by reinforcing the importance of participation (such as providing teachers with additional preparation time in their classes to complete research-related tasks or providing rewards for classes that return information by a deadline). Exhibit 1.1 provides a list of ways in which principals may help increase investment of their school stakeholders.

Exhibit 1.1

Ways Principals Can Increase Investment by Their School Stakeholders

1. Send letters on school letterhead explaining the goals and methods of the project to all school stakeholders. This shows that the school is supporting the program.
2. Hold evening open houses to introduce the researchers to the school stakeholders (or invite researchers to already-planned events, such as Back-to-School Night).
3. Sponsor contests to see which class can return the most informed consent forms or surveys. (People who do not want to participate can turn in blank forms with their signature, so that a class is not penalized if someone chooses not to participate.)
4. Provide teachers with extra preparation time on weeks when their participations is at a higher-than-normal level.
5. Disseminate research information (e.g., deadlines, results) in school newsletters, on their Web sites, or during daily announcement times in school.

Benefits for Principals and Schools

Another key to program success is the researcher's ability to articulate a study's benefits for schools and principals. Unless principals can see the benefits of partnering with a research program, they are not likely to risk disrupting the working balance of their school. Researchers and principals can work together to identify needs that exist within the school system and then find ways to apply research program resources to address these needs. For example, researchers may be able to use their expertise to provide advice, information, or interventions that benefit parents, school employees, and students. If such strategies are implemented, researchers should be careful that their actions do not alter the school context in ways that might bias their findings (e.g., provide such services when the project is finished). Additionally, professional development seminars or open houses for parents facilitated by academic professionals may be advantageous. Moreover, research teams may be able to answer questions that are important to individual schools by including additional assessments within their instrumentation. These answers can then be appropriately distributed to people who can use it best, such as teachers, guidance counselors, and parents.

Another way researchers can benefit schools is by sharing financial resources. For instance, researchers may procure funds to provide school supplies in return for the time and energy a school invests in a research program. Researchers might also be able to pay honoraria to school staff members, such as classroom teachers, aides, or secretaries who gather information for researchers. Financial incentives such as these should be taken into consideration when researchers devise budgets for their projects.

Open communication between principals and researchers can also result in a reduction in the workload required of school personnel throughout the research process. When principals and researchers are able to discuss the types of assessments that are routinely conducted within a school system, whether through in-house assessments, through federally mandated assessments, or from partnerships with other research programs, plans for data collection can be streamlined to reduce the risk of fatigue effect on school employees. Furthermore, these conversations can assist in scheduling data collection processes so as to not interfere with the busiest times of the school year.

Teachers

Many researchers rely on teachers as a pivotal data source for their research projects. For those who intend to work with teachers, it is crucial to recognize that teachers have very demanding jobs and that much of their work is done outside regular class hours. A teacher's chief duties include (a) designing and implementing instructional activities, (b) helping to create course curriculums, (c) providing classroom management, (d) maintaining public relations (e.g., parents, staff members), (e) attending in-service and professional growth activities, and (f) providing student evaluations.[2] In sum, teachers are responsible for the education, development, and well-being of their students—all of which are challenging tasks. Researchers must respect that teachers have little free time in their day and that their work can be overwhelming.

Working With Teachers

In addition to serving as research informants (e.g., completing interviews or surveys), teachers often act as the liaison between a research program and other school stakeholders. Thus, it is essential for researchers to fully communicate the goals of the program to teachers and address any concerns that reduce teacher buy-in. Teachers can set the tone for a project; they are usually the ones who present the research program to their students, and students are often the ones who discuss the project with their parents. Furthermore, teachers may also agree to collect completed informed consent forms and surveys from students and parents. Therefore, research participation levels are often in the hands of classroom teachers.

Beyond recruitment and class participation, researchers often rely on teachers as sources of information. For instance, teachers are experts on their classrooms and can help researchers determine the best time to gather data in this context (e.g., a teacher might know whether their students concentrate better before or after recess). When collecting data in classrooms, teachers can help to manage children's behavior during the

---

[2] Sample job descriptions for open teacher positions often highlight the themes noted as being central to the career. The Polk County Public Schools in Florida provide a nice example, which can be seen at http://www.polk-fl.net/employment/.

data collection process. Not only are teachers the best sources of information about their students, but they often have wonderful relationships with their students' parents. This allows them to provide feedback on topics such as the best research incentives to choose for students and parents (e.g., whether local water park tickets are more desired than movie tickets), and whether there are key parents within the classroom who can help motivate other parents to participate.

Valuing Teachers and Building a Legacy

In our conversations with teachers and other school personnel, one of the most common reasons given for not agreeing to work with researchers on school-based projects was that they felt shortchanged or "used" by previous investigators. Too often, it seems, researchers have tended to rely on teachers and other school personnel to conduct their studies but have not given credit to these individuals for their contributions or incorporated these individuals into the knowledge-production and dissemination phases of their projects. It is easy for researchers to forget that, along with other school personnel, teachers are often central to the success of their projects and that these individuals should be informed about findings and potential applications of the results (if any). Although researchers might argue that many factors work against sharing results in a timely way (e.g., data analyses, publication lags), it is easy to see how school personnel become dissatisfied. Finding ways to present preliminary findings, especially ones that are interesting to school partners (but that will not bias ongoing projects), might help to alleviate some of this dissatisfaction. Close attention to the legacy a research program is building not only positively affects the success of the ongoing research project but also paves the way for future school-based research programs.

Another observation that emerged from these conversations was that teachers' willingness to participate in a research project and the level of effort they were willing to invest in a project were closely linked to the extent to which they felt valued by researchers. How researchers present or frame their studies can convey different meanings to teachers about their roles and importance in a project. Researchers who frame teachers' roles as "data clerks" should expect different responses compared with teachers who are made to feel that they are (on some level) collaborators in the project. A recent interview with school stakeholders who participated in the Pathways Project reinforced this point. When Principal Diane Hampel of Liberty Elementary School was asked, "What made your experience of working with a school-based research program a positive one?" her first response was that "it felt like people valued your time." Thus, it is crucial to send the message to teachers that their time and efforts are valued.

Researchers can convey this message in a variety of ways. First, they can appreciate that teachers are volunteers and are not required to participate in research, regardless of whether upper-level school administrators have approved of a project. Expressing appreciation to teachers when they lend a helping hand goes a long way. Thanking them verbally, with appropriate honoraria, or financially reimbursing them for their time (see Exhibit 1.2) is appropriate when teachers do things such as managing children's behavior while researchers collect data, reminding students to return informed consent forms, or obtaining surveys or other research materials from parents. These acts of gratitude can prevent teachers (and other school personnel) from feeling shortchanged.

Exhibit 1.2

Financially Reimbursing Teachers

It is appropriate to financially reimburse teachers for their time (e.g., for filling out surveys or for being interviewed), but it is often difficult to determine how much to budget for this cost. At the Pathways Project, we estimate the number of hours we are asking teachers to invest per task. Then we reimburse teachers at a rate that is similar to an average teacher's wage. Feedback from teachers who had previously been a part of the Pathways Project indicated that they most remembered that the project valued their time, and that they knew this because they were paid a professional wage for their efforts. School-based researchers should not underestimate these costs when devising their budget, as it is not unusual for them to constitute a significant portion of a researcher program's operating budget.

Exactly how teachers should be honored for their participation warrants researchers' consideration and creativity. Investigators may mean well by handing out "#1 Teacher" mugs to faculty before the holiday break, but the message of appreciation may be lost on the teacher who has a cabinet full of mugs from years and years of students (or from previous researchers!). Listening carefully to teachers' laments, observing the classroom supply status, or even asking teachers about the types of honoraria they would appreciate are good ways to ensure that gifts are truly meaningful. During the interview mentioned previously, Diane Hampel noted that she particularly appreciated when the Pathways Project provided funds to be used for classroom supplies, alleviating the need to purchase classroom "extras" out of her own pocket. Small gestures such as these can go a long way in building and maintaining relationships with school faculty.

Nonteaching Personnel

As with every other school employee, nonteaching personnel, or support staff, can play a significant role in the success or failure of a research program. Interaction with support staff can occur in a variety of ways, and many times these exchanges can be more informal (but just as respectful) than those undertaken with teachers or administrators. For example, administrative assistants are often responsible for scheduling principals' and superintendents' schedules, and they can be instrumental in setting up meetings between school personnel and researchers. Administrative assistants often are in charge or enforcing the school rules/state regulations that require visitors to sign in and out of the building. Additionally, sometimes administrative assistants are the only persons who can contact teachers when they are in their classrooms. For these and other reasons, administrative assistants can be an extremely helpful resource to researchers.

One model for working with administrative assistants is to create an arrangement with a school's administration about the types of services these persons will provide for researchers (e.g., contacting teachers, preparing class rosters, photocopying surveys) and the compensation that they will receive for the delivery of these services. Whether this or another approach is used, the establishment of relationships and clear expectations between researchers and support staff is often essential to making the research process move along smoothly and can alleviate stress on researchers and school personnel alike.

Finally, administrative assistants are an important source of information about events that affect project operations. It is through these persons that researchers typically learn about school closings, holiday breaks, teacher conferences, field trips, standardized testing schedules, and many other happenings that can jeopardize the best-laid data collection plans. Other nonteaching personnel, such as custodial and security staff, are also valuable to researchers. These staff members may assist with tasks such as gaining access to school facilities, locating supplies (e.g., tables, desks), and setting up lab equipment. Thus, the suggestions previously made in terms of valuing other school stakeholders hold equally true for support staff.

Students

One of the main reasons why researchers want to conduct studies in schools is because they are interested in having students serve as research participants. Thus, researchers must also build relationships with students to ensure the success of their projects. Cultivating student involvement is important, not just for data-gathering purposes but also because students tend to be the driving force in whether their parents remember to return informed consent forms, return project surveys, and so on. There are a variety of ways to build relationships with students.

For those who wish to work directly with students, research ethics (see chap. 2, this volume) require that investigators seek students' assent in addition to obtaining informed consent from their parent or guardian. Clearly communicating the risks and benefits, methods, and right to terminate participation at any time is mandatory. Ethical guidelines also require researchers to evaluate rewards and incentives to ensure that they are not manipulative in any way. It should never be difficult for a student to pass up participating because he or she would have to turn down a reward. For instance, many adolescents would have trouble turning down the reward of winning a video game console and might participate even if they felt uncomfortable with the requirements of a research program.

The importance of valuing participants' time and collaboration applies as much to students as it does to other school personnel. Such appreciation can be expressed in numerous ways through both tangible and intangible rewards. Care should be taken to ensure that rewards and incentives are developmentally appropriate. Asking classroom teachers for suggestions or seeking input from the students themselves may help researchers identify gifts that would be most appropriate for student participants. However, because the appropriateness of certain types of rewards may differ from one school to another (depending on their unique cultures), the researchers' choices should be referenced against school and parental preferences. If studies continue across school years (e.g., longitudinal studies), incentives or rewards for student participation should be offered in increments and adjusted for their developmental appropriateness. For example, in the Pathways Project, the gifts that were provided to children, preadolescents, and adolescents consisted of pencils and stickers, gift cards to electronic stores, and monetary checks, respectively.

It is both feasible and effective to thank student participants at the classroom level as well. Contests for pizza parties and school supplies can serve as a reminder for students to return informed consent forms (whether they are participating or not) and surveys, and they are a fun way to increase the student buy-in to a research program. The Pathways Project discovered that sending birthday cards to students from the research staff and providing magnets with project contact information printed on them were two effective way to maintain contact and participation.

Parents

Working with parents is a necessary part of school-based research because investigators need parental consent for students' participation, and they often wish to obtain project-related data from children's family members.

Most often, researchers go about these aims by calling or meeting with parents or by sending parent questionnaires to children's homes. Each of these methods for working with parents has inherent advantages and disadvantages; therefore, it is important to consider how researchers can build successful relationships with parents.

The most common way in which researchers communicate with parents is via written communication, usually in the form of an introduction letter, an informed consent letter, and instructions for data collection processes. Written communication allows parents and researchers to have a record of the details of the study, project timelines, and contact information. Furthermore, the same information can be sent to hundreds of parents at the same time, making the process efficient for researchers. Unfortunately, trying to explain all of the details associated with a research project can be cumbersome, and even well-intentioned parents may not have the time or patience to read a lengthy packet of papers.

One way to reduce the strain on parents is to provide brief, reader-friendly introduction letters. These letters should be kept to a single page, be written at middle-school level for easy reading, and include bold type and underlines to highlight important information. The prose should be warm and inviting and should provide multiple methods for contacting the researcher(s). Our experiences show that having a standard letterhead or research project logo helps parents "brand" or identify the project and enables them to better recognize and distinguish it within future correspondence. These letters cannot be used instead of a formal informed consent letter. Ethical and legal guidelines must always be followed closely (see chap. 2, this volume). However, letters of introduction can prepare parents (expectations, understanding) for the information that is contained in an informed consent letter.

Many times teachers send written communication home with students. This procedure is efficient for researchers and ensures that all parents receive the information at the same time. Shortcomings, however, are that researchers must rely on busy teachers to remember to hand out and collect materials, and rely on students to be responsible in delivering the paperwork to and from parents and teachers. One way to circumnavigate these concerns is to mail postage-paid information packets to students' homes. Although this method requires keeping updated records of students' addresses and paying for postage, the cost and effort may be worth it if teachers and students are not able or willing to take on these tasks. Open communication with teachers may help researchers determine the best communication strategy.

Another limitation of written communication is that it does not build personal rapport with parents. Given past abuses, parents may be justifiably leery of researchers' attempts to gather information about their families. Greater trust may be achieved when parents are able to ask questions, get a sense of the researchers' intentions, and place a face with the project's name. Of course, arranging face-to-face meetings with parents can be difficult (more so in some school districts than others). Principals and teachers may be able to offer advice about whether parent meetings are a reasonable venture. For schools with highly committed families, asking principals to call a town hall meeting or arranging to meet parents during an open house might be an appropriate avenue for parent contacts. In other schools, setting up a table or booth at a sporting event might be the most effective way to meet parents. Most likely, the researcher's creativity and feedback from school personnel will result in a successful plan.

As with all participants, researchers must make parents feel that they are valued contributors. Simple thank-you notes or phone calls or paying parents for their time can be effective ways of informing parents that they are valued. For longitudinal projects, having an increasing pay scale as years pass can help reduce attrition and increase parent buy-in.

Finally, building rapport with parents can make a difference in the success of a research program. One of the ways that the Pathways Project staff realized that a high level of parental involvement had been achieved was when some of the participants' parents began to call our office and ask when the next round of data would be collected. Many of these parents indicated that they were looking forward to their next contact with project personnel. Among the benefits of this type of rapport is that it reduces participant loss through attrition (e.g., parents are more motivated to update their contact information when they change addresses) and increases response rates to project surveys.

BUILDING RELATIONSHIPS:
TOP DOWN VERSUS BOTTOM UP

The discussion of school stakeholders within this chapter began with administrators and ended with parents. This structure was designed to parallel the typical organization chart of a school district (see Figure 1.1). However, this should not be interpreted to imply that relationships should be pursued or built from the top down. The process of relationship building in schools should begin with those that the researcher believes will most appropriately and effectively expand his or her network of connections. For example, if a researcher were familiar with the members of a Parents and Teachers Association (PTA), then it would be reasonable for this investigator to strengthen these relationships and allow motivated and interested PTA members to talk about the research program with other interested school personnel. Partnerships with schools might also begin through ties with parents. This may also help to gain the investment of other parents and teachers, alleviating some of the researcher's workload.

At the Pathways Project's inception, the staff members devised a unique method for building rapport with schools and increasing stakeholder's commitment to the project. The director met with principals from numerous school districts and talked with them about the value of beginning a long-term study of the predictors of children's scholastic and psychosocial achievement. Ideas about how the project might be conducted, including potential aims, methodologies, and timelines, were discussed, along with the benefits of partnering to achieve these goals. Specific benefits to schools were outlined, including access to study results; incentives for students, teachers, parents, and schools (e.g., honoraria for participation); access to experts; and the opportunity to include assessments that were relevant to individual schools. Then they created an application process in which interested schools could apply to join in partnership with the Pathways Project. School personnel were given the opportunity to express what they were prepared to invest in the program, how long they wanted to participate, and what conditions they would set for timelines, survey topics, and ways in which information could be disseminated.

Partnerships were undertaken with schools that had aims, requirements, and resources that achieved the best fit with those of the Pathways Project. Thus, this approach attempted to maximize the fit between the schools chosen and the research team and project. Both parties entered the partnership as motivated participants with similar goals and levels of investment. Our interviews with former school participants indicate that they felt valued by the researchers in the program and felt the process was worthwhile.

TRAINING YOUR RESEARCH TEAM TO BUILD RECIPROCAL RELATIONSHIPS

Research conducted in schools is a multifaceted, complex endeavor. Regardless of a project's size, organizational challenges exist. Small-scale projects may seem easier to manage, but with fewer people to complete the project, it is often necessary for staff members to play many roles. Large-scale research programs may be staffed by as many as 30 to 40 people. Supervising a large research program is not unlike running a small business, requiring a skill set that is often not included in traditional research methodology training. Thus, it is not enough for a principal investigator (PI) to consider and implement "best practices" (as illustrated in this volume); rather, the PI must know how to find qualified research staff and train them to work dependably in partnership with schools. This section discusses how to do just that.

PIs quickly learn the importance of creating both highly skilled and cooperative research teams. Teams typically bring together individuals with differing levels of experience and qualifications and may include senior or principal investigators, postdoctoral fellows, graduate research assistants, staff research assistants, and undergraduate students. This diversity of talent is often essential, but for teams to function effectively, PIs or project managers must identify each assistant's skills and motivate the team members to use these skills cooperatively or as part of a team effort.

Interpersonal or relationship skills are an important asset for most team members because these people act as the project's representatives when they contact or work in schools. A team member who is going into the schools will potentially interact with every type of stakeholder. For example, during a routine data collection trip to a school, a team member might check in with the administrative assistant, say good morning to the principal, ask for help in carrying equipment from the custodial staff, request permission to enter a classroom from a teacher, and explain to students the informed consent forms (that were approved by the school board). With each of these contacts, a team member has the opportunity to build or harm a relationship. Thus, it is important to evaluate each member in terms of his or her ability to interrelate with others.

The process of teaching team members to value participants and view schools as partners should be modeled and encouraged throughout a project's operation—from start to finish. This kind of interpersonal sensitivity can also be a criterion for staff selection. For example, rather than select student assistants or volunteers solely on the basis of their grade point averages and resumes, we suggest including an interview that probes their willingness to respect research collaborators and participants and their desire to work cooperatively in school contexts.

Before entering schools, it is sound practice to provide all team members with comprehensive training that includes instruction in topics such as the project's goals and methodology (not just the person's assigned task), protocol for responding to questions from participants and nonparticipants, rights of human subjects, confidentiality rules, requirements for data safety and protection, and procedures for reporting unexpected research incidents to the project's managers and/or IRB. Team members should be encouraged to wear project badges and carry business cards when traveling to schools and working with school personnel. To ensure that team members are competent at these tasks and skills, mock role-plays and other types of performance tests can be conducted before staff is assigned to schools.

Finally, although it may seem trivial, it is often important for members of research teams to respect schools' dress codes. It has been our experience that many team members (especially undergraduate and graduate students) need to be shown what it means to dress appropriately (i.e., professionally) for school visits. Many schools have expectations, and in some cases, explicit codes for teachers' and children's dress. In such cases it is a priority for visitors (team members) to respect these expectations and dress appropriately. For large-scale research programs that will have team members in the school environment on a regular basis, PIs may consider establishing a project dress code that resembles or matches that of the schools in which staff members will visit or work.

Another key to staff management is coping with turnover. Researchers who wish to maintain high levels of productivity will want to plan for anticipated personnel changes, such as when students enter and leave the team across academic years, so that experienced members can be used to train new members. Pairing team members with others of varying levels of expertise allows the more advanced members the chance to try their hand at mentoring, and the novices to have a safe person to come to when they do not know the answer to a question.

For the Pathways Project, the benefits of training team members became so clear that a for-credit university course was created for all entry-level team members. This allowed for standardization in the training process and ensured that each of the concepts described above were covered. Prior to joining the Pathways Project, each team member had to demonstrate proficiency in all areas of the training module via written tests and role-playing. This strategy is recommended, as it was highly successful.

CONCLUSION

We intend for this chapter to be a practical guide to building successful relationships with school stakeholders. Every researcher who enters a school leaves a legacy. This chapter's purpose is to help researchers build a legacy that they can be proud of—one that builds a foundation of goodwill upon which future partnerships can be established. We believe that the way to do this is by building relationships with all types of school stakeholders. We challenge researchers to invest in partnerships that benefit both schools and researchers. We encourage school-based researchers to approach their potential school partners with preparedness, especially knowing who the school stakeholders are within the district and the unique role they play. Finally, we encourage researchers to use creativity and open communication to build a strong relationship foundation.

Infusing the importance of working *with* instead of conducting research *on* schools into all aspects of a school-based research program will lead to successful school-based research programs in the present and for future research programs to come.

REFERENCES

Ladd, G. W. (2005). *Children's peer relationships and social competence: A century of progress.* New Haven, CT: Yale University Press.

National Association of Elementary School Principals. (2001). *Leading learning communities: NAESP standards for what principals should know and be able to do.* Alexandria, VA: Author.

Parkay, F. W., & Stanford, B. H. (1998). *Becoming a teacher.* Boston: Allyn & Bacon.

2

Navigating Institutional Review Boards When Conducting School-Based Research

Mari Strand Cary

The American Educational Research Association reminds its members to "respect the rights, privacy, dignity, and sensitivities of their research populations and also the integrity of the institutions within which the research occurs" (Strike et al., 2002, p. 43). Respecting and, in fact, protecting the population participating in research studies is a crucial part of conducting sound research and maintaining the public's trust in research. All researchers must honestly and painstakingly evaluate and disclose the nature of proposed research and the potential impact on its participants. This is especially true for those working with vulnerable populations, such as when school-based researchers work with children in school settings when parents are not, by default, directly involved. It is not enough to conduct research carefully. Researchers must also conduct research ethically according to three principles outlined in "The Belmont Report: Ethical Principles and Guidelines for the Protection of Human Subjects of Research": respect for persons, beneficence, and justice (Office for Protection From Research Risks, 1979).

Federal mandates require that researchers respect and protect research populations. Title 45 Code of Federal Regulations Part 46 (45 CFR 46, also called the Common Rule) requires review and approval of federally funded research involving human subjects by the researchers' institutional review board (IRB). These local boards review proposed and ongoing studies to ensure that researchers are taking appropriate steps to protect study participants' rights and welfare. As research in schools has become more commonplace, many pre-K–12 schools have formal review processes or IRBs that mirror those found in universities or within federally regulated IRBs. This chapter begins by addressing the purpose of IRBs and what they look for when approving research.

It is often the case that researchers encounter difficulties trying to coordinate the university and school approval processes. Sometimes, researchers must gain university approval before school approval. Other times, school approval must be procured first. There are even circumstances when the researcher faces the seemingly impossible task of getting approval when neither the university nor school is willing to approve first! Time, extensive communication, and finesse on the part of the researcher are required to move beyond approval impasses. The second part of the chapter provides general strategies for researchers hoping to establish partnerships with schools and conduct school-based research. These strategies apply to both university and school approval processes. Additionally, throughout the entire chapter, the reader will encounter the types of questions researchers can ask themselves and others, resources to draw on, actions to take, and difficulties to anticipate as they formally or informally seek project approval to do research in pre-K–12 schools.

The remainder of the chapter provides university- and school-specific information and suggestions. Researchers may find these particularly useful as they seek approval of their school-based research designs and strive to establish successful school partnerships (see Exhibit 2.1).

Exhibit 2.1

Implications of IRB Approval

Regardless of how easy or difficult it is to procure IRB approval or approval from the schools themselves, Lisa Dinella reminds school-based researchers that "IRB approval does not imply that a study is well-designed or will yield useful data. Approval only means that, based on what the researchers have said they are planning to do, the decision makers are confident that the researcher is proceeding ethically" (L. M. Dinella, personal communication, September 25, 2007).

WHAT ARE IRBS, AND WHAT DO THEY REQUIRE?

Before IRBs existed, researchers decided both the goals and methods of studies with little or no oversight. Historically, human experimentation by Nazi physicians and scientists and, on U.S. soil, studies such as the Tuskegee syphilis experiment (1932–1972) played pivotal roles in drawing attention to abusive research practices. IRBs were created in response to such abuses conducted in the name of research. For example, in 1946 the Nuremberg Code was developed as a way for the Nuremberg Military Tribunals to judge Nazi human experimentation, the Declaration of Helsinki was adopted by the World Medical Association in 1964, and, in 1975 the United States signed the National Research Act into law (Miser, 2005). In subsequent years, U.S. federal regulations for the protection of human subjects were revised and expanded, and in 1979 the Belmont Report was published (Office for Protection From Research Risks, 1979) outlining basic ethical principles decided on by a federal commission. As mentioned, these provided a strong foundation for the federally mandated 45 CFR 46.

IRBs are required by the U.S. Department of Health and Human Services for "all research involving human subjects conducted, supported or otherwise subject to regulation by any federal department or agency" (45 CFR 46.101). Thus, these boards now exist, under various names, at academic institutions, medical facilities, and some for-profit companies. According to these guidelines, IRBs must be independent of the researchers and have a diverse membership (i.e., size, experience, gender, profession, affiliation). Most important, in accordance with 45 CFR 46, IRBs only approve research that minimizes risks to subjects, provides a reasonable risk-to-benefit ratio, equitably selects subjects, receives and documents informed consent, monitors data to ensure subject safety, protects privacy and data confidentiality, and provides additional safeguards to protect the rights and welfare of subjects likely to be vulnerable to coercion or undue influence (e.g., children, prisoners, pregnant women, mentally disabled persons, economically or educationally disadvantaged persons).

Information regarding the history, issues, guidelines, ethical principles, and vocabulary inherent to IRBs—including links to the Belmont Report, Declaration of Helsinki, and Nuremberg Code—may be found on the Office for Human Research Protections Web site (http://www.hhs.gov/ohrp).

Also, articles and reports by Miser (2005), Eissenberg et al. (2006), Hemmings (2006), and the Center for Advanced Study (2005) are particularly useful and accessible.

GENERAL STRATEGIES FOR SCHOOL-BASED RESEARCHERS

Researchers hoping to conduct school-based studies should act in such a way as to benefit the education community, school, university, and research program in the immediate and foreseeable future. To do this, researchers can design valuable studies, respect those involved, overestimate the time required to complete the study, be well-informed, submit complete applications and monitor their approval, and document the entire process.

Validate the Research as Necessary and Informative

The first step school-based researchers should take in seeking university or school approval to conduct research in school settings is to validate that the proposed research is necessary and informative to the research program and community and, more important, partner schools and the education community. The following are important considerations:

- *Is the idea sound? Has appropriate piloting of materials and approaches been conducted?* Research based on false assumptions or inappropriately structured materials is unlikely to be successful or useful and may, in fact, be detrimental (e.g., resulting in ungrounded recommendations or decisions). Researchers and their partner schools waste valuable time that could instead be devoted to quality research or educational efforts. Worse, broad, long-lasting decisions regarding interventions, teaching approaches, and lessons may be made on the basis of flawed data. Such outcomes further neither school nor researcher goals.
- *Is the school setting necessary?* Even if schools are interested in a particular line of research, they cannot allow school-based researchers to conduct studies that divert substantial energy from the educational process or put students at unreasonable risk. Restricting requests to only those projects that require the school setting shows respect for schools' time

and resources as well as other members of the educational research community. On a practical level, researchers must also consider the costs and benefits of working in the schools. Conducting the research in schools may not add any value above and beyond that which could be gained through a more efficient, cost-effective, and/or more controlled laboratory study.

- *Are the expected effect sizes of proposed interventions or instructional methods worth the investment required of the school stakeholders? Would the results be compelling enough for a community to make significant changes based on the findings?* If the answer to either question is no, perhaps the study would be better suited for a laboratory study. These laboratory studies could eventually lead to school-based studies in which the effects could be expected to be more dramatic or meaningful.

Convey Respect

To successfully build research partnerships with schools, effectively navigate approval processes, and reduce confusion and stress of future applications, researchers should strive for positive interactions with officials and staff at every level. Treating others with respect, being friendly and professional, and following through with promised phone calls, e-mails, and application materials will result in greater interest, responsiveness, and accommodation from all stakeholders and individuals involved in the approval process. This is particularly crucial when communicating with school personnel. Researchers must remember that schools are under no obligation to allow on-site research. Whereas many universities include research as one of their missions, that is certainly not the case with schools. Their sole mission is the education of their students. As noted in chapter 1 of this volume, respect truly is a cornerstone of successful researcher–school research partnerships.

Overestimate the Time Needed to Gain Project Approval and Conduct the Study

School-based researchers should have realistic expectations about when they will conduct their studies in the chosen schools. Schools and university

IRBs vary in how quickly they review projects and provide feedback to researchers, and what types of resubmit processes and timelines are available to researchers if a study is not approved when first submitted. Even if schools are excited about research partnerships, researchers may need to enter the schools months or even a year later than expected owing to the duration of review processes, the pre-K–12 academic calendar, and unanticipated delays. Study durations are also often much lengthier than anticipated. Furthermore, to maintain educational standards, districts or schools often explicitly prohibit research during certain times of the year (see Bernatek, 2007, for an example). School-based researchers often consider the official school calendar while planning their studies (thus accommodating vacations, in-service days, half-days, and standardized testing days) but are unaware of unofficial events (e.g., test preparation days, field trips, or days when students are deemed by teachers to be least likely to be attentive). To minimize lengthy delays, especially unanticipated ones, school-based researchers should collect information from many different sources (particularly classroom teachers, when appropriate). This will enable them to determine realistically timed data collection periods that accomplish research goals while minimizing inconvenience to the school.

Be Well-Informed Before Choosing a Study Design and Submitting an Application

Successfully establishing research partnerships with schools largely depends on understanding university and school approval processes, fitting projects to particular schools, and developing positive, mutually beneficial relationships with school stakeholders.

University Approval Process Information

One way school-based researchers can make educated guesses about the time it will take to start and conduct studies is to be well informed about the approval procedures and the schools likely to be involved. Researchers should begin by understanding how their home institution handles IRB issues. Although universities usually have extensive documentation detailing their IRB processes and make this information readily available through

Web sites and IRB information sessions, an often underused resource is the university's IRB liaisons or compliance officers. Before, during, and after the approval process, these individuals can help the researcher determine what is really necessary for a particular project, act proactively to provide details or information the review committee will need, and, if the project is not approved, understand why, so that subsequent, revised applications meet with success.

School Approval Process Information

Similarly, school-based researchers must fully understand the approval procedures of the schools (e.g., required materials and deadlines, key personnel, times of year when research is not allowed). Again, researchers can begin by investigating the school or district's Web site and other publicly available materials, knowing that vocabulary, personnel titles, and jurisdiction over research approvals vary greatly from school to school.

School Characteristics and Culture

Knowing schools' approval process details is not enough, however. As discussed throughout this volume, to establish successful partnerships with schools, researchers must also be familiar with the characteristics of those schools. School size, demographics, and test score information are important, of course, but more illuminating and helpful are organizational structure, new initiatives and areas of concern, areas of emphasis (e.g., drama, math/science, cultural awareness), involvement with the community, and participation in research. Test-score reporting Web sites, national Web sites reviewing school districts, and local news articles can often provide these insights. It is useful to speak with colleagues who have experience working with the proposed school stakeholders. Such established educational researchers can provide introductions to school stakeholders, make recommendations on how best to present a research proposal, share examples of how they have integrated school priorities and interests, or suggest particular schools that would be a good fit for the study.

If by doing all of the above the school-based researcher has found little information and does not know how to move forward, he or she can call the school or district directly and ask who to contact for information about conducting education research in the schools. Not surprisingly, administrators tend to appreciate researchers' efforts to educate themselves before starting such conversations (see Exhibit 2.2).

Cultivate Valuable Liaisons

Regardless of how well researchers have gathered information, it is always productive to build on existing personal or professional relationships and identify individuals affiliated with the school system who can act as liaisons between the researchers and the school. These "gatekeepers" are invaluable to both schools and researchers because they truly understand how school systems work and thus can increase the efficiency and productiveness of communication between the two (see Exhibit 2.3). Not surprisingly, individuals with research backgrounds are particularly good gatekeepers because they are sympathetic to the research endeavor and understand many of the issues and constraints inherent to research. Given

---

Exhibit 2.2

The Advantage of Face-to-Face Meetings

Chris Schunn, associate professor of psychology at the University of Pittsburgh, encourages researchers to arrange face-to-face meetings whenever possible. In an approval process that often hinges on personal relations, "e-mail or letters or phone calls won't cut it." Information revealed informally during face-to-face meetings (but that would never come up in a quick phone call or e-mail exchange) can dramatically alter a study's chance of approval. For example, a district employee who is aware of research activities and is accountable to a variety of parties might mention that altering the grade levels involved in the study or changing the project description's vocabulary will cause the proposed study to fall under the jurisdiction of research that was already approved or will nicely complement existing school initiatives. The researcher would do well to incorporate those changes (C. D. Schunn, personal communication, June 11, 2007).

Exhibit 2.3

Gatekeepers as Valuable Liaisons

Judith Touré, assistant professor of education, Carlow University, experienced the power of gatekeepers during her dissertation work. After frustrating false starts in one district, she contacted a friend of hers who was a young principal in the Pittsburgh Public Schools. The principal was interested in Judith's topic and provided her with the names of several other district principals who would likely support the study. The principal went even further by contacting those principals ahead of time so that Judith's later calls were not a surprise. Those principals, in turn, served as gatekeepers to other key school personnel. Judith also found an unexpected gatekeeper in one school: The parent liaison (a staff member charged with ensuring open communication between parents and the school) was in the building much of the time, had an open schedule, and was quick to respond to e-mails. For this reason, that parent liaison could easily provide information Judith desperately needed on a day-to-day basis, for example, up-to-date school schedules and the best way to find and talk with particular individuals (J. Touré, personal communication, July 6, 2007).

the value of relationships between researchers and these individuals, cultivating relationships with school and district employees should be one of a school-based researcher's top priorities. In some cases, gatekeepers truly make the difference between a successful project and long-lasting research relationship and one that does not even survive the approval process. Again, more detailed information about such relationship building may be found in chapter 1.

Submit Complete Approval Applications and Stay Involved

How does a school-based researcher actually obtain approval from both the university and school once the research design has been detailed and necessary planning and relationship building is completed? This section highlights materials researchers should be prepared to submit and actions that may smooth the application's way through the approval processes.

Materials to Prepare and Have Readily Available

In general, researchers should prepare the same types of materials, regardless of the approval process. Although the materials might not be required for an official application, they might be useful in a different context. Though formats will vary, researchers should have the following materials available:

- proof of IRB approval (or application status) from the researcher's home institution and/or from the school, if available and applicable;
- contact information for key members of the research team;
- one- to two-page description of study's purpose and design in laypersons' terms;
- detailed description of proposed participants and how they will be selected;
- expected benefits to participants and school(s);
- plans for protection of data and dissemination of results (e.g., assigning random identification numbers to students so that data may be kept in a separate file from the associated student names or school identification numbers);
- anticipated means of disseminating results;
- letters of support from teachers, principals, and administrators (if available);
- security clearances for each team member (necessary when working in schools);
- information letters that will be distributed to participants and other stakeholders;
- consent/assent forms (in the language of the person to whom they are addressed) and the plan for explaining the study to participants, ensuring participants understand they can withdraw without penalty, and procuring consent and assent (whether written or verbal);

- instructional materials/scripts, assessments, questionnaires, observation procedures, and why they are necessary;
- list of needs (e.g., access to standardized test scores, rooms, expected data collection dates, expected completion date) and justifications for them; and
- situation- or application-specific materials.

Continuing to Be Involved After Submitting the Application

Having submitted their applications, school-based researchers sometimes believe they have done all they can do to procure project approval. Yet researchers need to remain engaged. It is useful for researchers to always know where in the approval process they stand, what needs to be done next, and whom to contact if questions or concerns arise. Whether these interactions are by e-mail, phone, fax, mail, or face-to-face meetings, researchers should keep a dated record of all incoming and outgoing correspondence and notes about conversations, copies of materials submitted, and copies of approvals. If materials or messages are lost in the daily administrative shuffle, office moves, or personnel changes, it is helpful to be able to resend them within hours. Accurate, detailed, easy-to-reference records will make the approval process proceed smoothly.

Leave a Positive Legacy

Finally, it is useful for school-based researchers to note successes (e.g., procuring particularly powerful letters of introduction, interacting with a helpful district secretary, receiving compliments on an easy-to-read study description) and failures (e.g., improper communications, proposal wording that confused or alarmed readers, overinvestment in schools that feigned interest, poor recordkeeping). Researchers' detailed notes about what to repeat, seek out, avoid completely, or do differently next time are immensely helpful to their laboratory, department, and education research colleagues. Though often available only through personal correspondence, such information is sometimes compiled at a department or even university level. Indeed, such mindfulness of the process behind school-based research led to the publishing of this volume!

NAVIGATING THE UNIQUE UNIVERSITY IRB CHALLENGES SCHOOL-BASED RESEARCHERS FACE

As noted earlier, the general intent of IRBs are the same from institution to institution. Nonetheless, actual procedures vary widely, and, as many researchers have found out, school-based research often suffers unanticipated delays during the university review process. Some reasons for this are that education research does not fit neatly into familiar research models (e.g., biomedical studies, psychology laboratory studies), its methods may be unfamiliar to those sitting on the IRB, and the definitions on which education research depends are interpreted differently by different people. When IRBs were established, "essentially everyone within that group knew what they were talking about. However . . . as the biomedical model was extrapolated to other disciplines, problems began to arise. Fuzzy terminology leads to fuzzy guidelines" (Center for Advanced Study, 2005, p. 8). Guidelines that seem straightforward in the generic sense become vague and difficult to adhere to when applied to a specific school-based study.

Should the IRB Play a Role?

One rather basic area of confusion to both researchers and IRBs is whether a particular project is subject to IRB approval in the first place. First and foremost, school-based researchers must remember that IRBs exist for research purposes. Nonresearch projects tend not to be subject to IRB review. Federal policy (45 CFR 46.102) defines research as "a systematic investigation, including research development, testing, and evaluation, designed to develop or to contribute to generalizable knowledge." Thus, some work educational researchers do may not, technically, be research. For example, instructional materials might be tested as part of a quality assurance study rather than through an evaluation or research study. That being said, even when a project is not research, does not involve human subjects, or would normally not need to be reviewed for another reason, a researcher's funders or institution might deem it subject to review.

Three Categories of IRB Review

Similarly, determining which of three IRB review categories is appropriate for a study is challenging even to seasoned researchers. The three categories of IRB review are *full board, expedited,* and *exempt.* If a study is not considered for exempt or expedited review, it is subject to a full board review. Expedited studies require review by only part of the board. This category often includes previously approved research (e.g., for minor changes or when data collection has not yet started), yet other activities might justify expedited status as well (see 45 CFR 46.110). School-based researchers will find the following most relevant: research involving materials that have been collected or will be collected solely for nonresearch purposes, collection of data from recordings made for research purposes, and research on individual or group characteristics or behavior or research using group-level methods. The treatment of exempt studies varies by university but constitutes the simplest review process. Again, many activities might justify exempt status (see 45 CFR 46.101), but the following are likely most relevant to school-based researchers: normal educational practices in established educational settings; educational tests, survey procedures, interview procedures or observation of public behavior; and collection or study of existing data. Researchers must remember that even if a study is deemed exempt from IRB review, researchers must still conduct research in an ethical manner.

Caught Up in the Details

Another challenge faced by all investigators, but particularly school-based researchers, is how much detail to provide in IRB applications. As a general rule, researchers will do well to avoid providing more detail than is required. "Choose very carefully which kinds of details you choose to be detailed in. . . . Ethics doesn't hinge on which version of the test you use and it is a waste of everyone's resources to pretend it does" (C. D. Schunn, personal communication, June 11, 2007). For example, if a school-based researcher provides excruciating detail about her participants, measures, and timelines, she is essentially locking herself into a research design that she may very well want or need to change by the time she actually gets approval by the schools to conduct the research.

If a researcher's study is likely to change before or during implementation (due to unexpected circumstances or because it is an intervention intended to change in response to changing participant needs or circumstances), the researcher should write the IRB accordingly (E. Cappella, personal communication, June 4, 2007). Similarly, if the researcher plans to continue in the same line of research for a number of years, it may be particularly useful to the researcher and the IRB to write the IRB broadly (e.g., large sample sizes, reference to included measures as "examples," broad study questions) so that each subsequent study design can be considered a part of the broader, already approved, design.

NAVIGATING SCHOOL APPROVAL PROCESSES FOR A SUCCESSFUL RESEARCH PARTNERSHIP

Researchers' timely success in establishing research partnerships often lies in knowing how administrators and educators feel about research and fully understanding how to navigate the approval process.

Interest in Research

A school's stance toward on-site research can provide an entry point for building relationships and frame the entire approval process. School professionals' primary goals and responsibilities center on educating students. Some teachers and administrators view research primarily as a chance for the school to contribute to, and benefit from, cutting-edge methods, materials, and ideas. Often on the basis of prior experience with researchers, other educators may feel research is a distraction from, and a hindrance to, school goals. Regardless of view, schools have put IRB-like processes in place to help administrators fully understand the research being conducted in their schools and, in many cases, to limit the number, scope, or content of research studies. Because not every research proposal is a good fit for every school, researchers need to be prepared for, and gracefully accept, a school's decision not to participate. School-based researchers will be more successful if they allow themselves enough time to present their research program to multiple schools or districts.

Formal Versus Informal Approval Procedures

As a general rule, school-based researchers can expect larger public school districts in close proximity to universities to have the most formal IRB procedures. They are more likely to be inundated with research requests and therefore need a means of dealing with such requests efficiently and fairly. In general, schools further from universities, smaller districts, private schools, and charter schools utilize less formal procedures. In fact, some of these schools may not have research approval protocols because they do not have the need or resources to implement formal procedures.

It is important to know that the existence of formal IRB-like processes implies neither a dismissal nor a welcoming of on-site research. Formality tends to bring with it clear guidelines, contact persons, and written agreements. Such characteristics are particularly useful for multiyear studies because approval will likely remain even as individual teachers or other participants move to other positions. With formality also comes potentially lengthier decision-making periods, school-suggested or required revisions to the research plan, and hierarchical bureaucracies to navigate. Engaging in formal review procedures allows administrators to be restrictive about what, if any research, they allow. Consequently, the requirements might be prohibitive (e.g., having year-long review processes or requiring 100% rate of return for consent forms before entering classrooms), or the rejection rate might be extremely high.

Types of Approval Processes

Approval processes can proceed from the top down, from the bottom up, or at multiple levels.

Approval From the Top Down

Schools with top-down approval processes require a full evaluation and a priori approval by appropriate governing boards and administration for any activities conducted by or for nonschool personnel. Sometimes this review is conducted formally through processes that mirror formal IRB processes. At other times face-to-face meetings or letters explaining the study are enough to gain approval by the main decision makers. Once high-level approval has been granted, school-based researchers should meet with principals of proposed partner schools and, finally, teachers or other school employees on whom the research depends. It is often the case that even when approval is granted at high levels, individual staff members can decide whether to take part in the study, thus these meetings are important to gaining full levels of participation. Sometimes, even when approval must come from the top, the final decision makers want to know researchers have spoken with and received partnership agreements from individual schools and teachers prior to engaging in the approval process.

Approval From the Bottom Up

On the other end of the spectrum are schools that retain a high degree of autonomy for themselves, their staff, and their teachers when it comes to deciding whether research can be conducted onsite. Gaining approval for a study in these cases largely rests on the researchers' abilities to establish relationships with the school stakeholders with whom they plan to work, and the researchers' abilities to accurately convey the value of the research being proposed. Early, voluntary, and committed involvement by staff (even when students are the focus of the study) improves and is often crucial to successful education studies. Conversations with teachers have the added benefit of identifying questions of interest in particular classrooms or student populations. Once school personnel tentatively commit to the project, it is appropriate for researchers to notify and/or request permission of upper-level administration. Researchers should be ready to explain and even alter their research methodology to meet the concerns and needs of these individuals.

Approval at Multiple Levels Simultaneously

In reality, schools tend not to have a clear top-down or bottom-up approval process. Working within the constraints of the school system tends to require school-based researchers to operate on several of levels simultaneously (e.g., finding out which teachers are interested if the researcher can obtain administrative approval while simultaneously gauging whether the district will approve the project if teachers agree to be involved). Additionally, school-based researchers often do informal recruiting months or years before starting formal review processes. In all circumstances, researchers must

> ## Exhibit 2.4
> **Approval at Multiple Levels Simultaneously**
>
> Eli Silk, a doctoral student at the Learning Research and Development Center, University of Pittsburgh, had the experience of working at multiple levels simultaneously. Having recruited an interested teacher, he drafted a letter of approval support that the teacher took to the principal to sign, along with a copy of the IRB proposals to the university and district. This bottom-up approach gave him some confidence as he struggled with the district's inaccessible, unclear, and lengthy top-down approval process. Although the project had not yet been approved by the district, Eli could confidently speak to the school's interest and ability to participate in the study. Members of the research team then worked closely with the district's IRB staff person to monitor the proposal's progress through the system (E. M. Silk, personal communication, June 1, 2007).

be careful not to upset stakeholders or sabotage relationships by giving the impression they are working outside established systems. Similarly, school-based researchers should never assume a request to conduct research will be approved, make promises (regarding timing, involvement, compensation) they might regret, or exaggerate the support they have to-date. Exhibit 2.4 provides an example of a doctoral student's experience seeking with approval at multiple levels simultaneously.

CONCLUSION

Although there is no guaranteed means of receiving approval to conduct research with pre-K–12 schools, there are certain practices that meet with a dramatically higher rate of success than others. Key to these are fully understanding the purpose, requirements, and procedures of applicable IRBs; proposing worthwhile research; respecting the time, expertise, and concerns of students, educators, administrators, and other stakeholders (largely covered in other chapters); overestimating the amount of time needed; establishing or strengthening relationships with school stakeholders; and carefully completing and monitoring the application process. This chapter has provided an overview of these successful practices as well as describing some of the obstacles that may be encountered as school-based researchers seek to partner with schools. This chapter has not explicitly emphasized the importance of ensuring proposed studies match well with potential partner schools, thus the reader is encouraged to see other chapters for those crucial discussions. By following the guidelines and developing answers to the questions presented in this chapter, researchers will be well prepared to successfully navigate university and school approval processes.

REFERENCES

Bernatek, B. (2007, December). *Guidelines for research projects in the Seattle Public Schools* (Revised ed.). Retrieved January 5, 2009, from http://www.seattle schools.org/area/siso/external_research/researchguidelines.pdf

Center for Advanced Study. (2005). *The Illinois white paper: Improving the system for protecting human subjects: Counteracting IRB "mission creep."* Retrieved March 13, 2008, from http://www.law.uiuc.edu/conferences/whitepaper

Code of Federal Regulations, Title 45: Public welfare, Part 46: Protection of human subjects. Revised June 23, 2005. Effective June 23, 2005. Washington, DC: U.S. Department of Health and Human Services.

Eissenberg, T., Panicker, S., Berenbaum, S., Epley, N., Fendrich, M., Kelso, R., et al. (2006). *IRBs and psychological science: Ensuring a collaborative relationship.* Washington, DC: American Psychological Association, Board of Scientific Affairs Working Group.

Hemmings, A. (2006). Great ethical divides: Bridging the gap between institutional review boards and researchers. *Educational Researcher, 35,* 12–18.

Miser, W. (2005). Educational research: To IRB, or not to IRB? *Family Medicine, 37,* 168–173.

Office for Protection From Research Risks, National Commission for the Protection of Human Subjects of Biomedical and Behavioral Research. (1979). *The Belmont report: Ethical principles and guidelines for the protection of human subjects of research* (GPO 887-809). Washington, DC: U.S. Government Printing Office.

Strike, K. A., Anderson, M. S., Curren, R., van Geel, T., Pritchard, I., & Robertson, E. (2002). *Ethical standards of the American Educational Research Association: Cases and commentary.* Washington, DC: American Educational Research Association.

3

Rigorous, Responsive, and Responsible: Experimental Designs in School Intervention Research

Elise Cappella, Greta M. Massetti, and Sasha Yampolsky

Schools in the United States are facing intense scrutiny. Standardized test scores remain stagnant and continue to lag in international comparisons, even though more U.S. students are graduating high school and attending college than before (National Center for Education Statistics, 2000; Snyder, Dillow, & Hoffman, 2007). Large gaps in achievement by student socioeconomic status, disability, and race/ethnicity exist, while at the same time public schools face the challenge—and opportunity—of an increasingly diverse student body across these domains and others (Federal Interagency Forum on Child & Family Statistics, 2007; U.S. Census Bureau, 2004). American society has become more globally oriented and technologically advanced, leading to an emphasis in recent years on producing citizens with high levels of education and skills, and accompanying attention to educational processes and outcomes (U.S. Department of Education, 2006).

Given this social and educational climate, schools and districts face pressure to increase the quality of educational experiences for all students. However, there is no consensus, as of yet, regarding the best ways to reform schools and build student achievement, particularly for groups of students who are lagging behind. Federal and state governments have

Greta M. Massetti is currently a behavioral scientist in the Centers for Disease Control and Prevention's Division of Violence Prevention.

become involved in the debate by (a) mandating the use of "evidence-based" or "scientifically rigorous" programs and curricula in schools and (b) providing resources and expertise to build capacity within schools and research communities to conduct the studies to generate those data (Porter & Polikoff, 2007; U.S. Department of Education, 2002). The No Child Left Behind Act of 2001 (NCLB) was the first to orient educators and researchers toward the importance of assessing educational experiences. Broadly speaking, NCLB requires that all programs and curricula implemented in schools have a research base that is "rigorous, systematic, and objective" (see Brass, Nunez-Neto, & Williams, 2006). Similar language has been used in subsequent reports, such as the 2002 report of the Coalition for Evidence-Based Policy advocating "rigorous study designs" in education research (Brass et al., 2006, pp. 12, 22; Eisenhart & Towne, 2003). Related initiatives, including the Education Sciences Reform Act and the Reading First Act, have allocated funds to support scientifically based curricula to improve the quality of education in general, and reading instruction in particular (Porter & Polikoff, 2007). In addition, state legislatures are increasingly involved in supporting so-called effective programs to buttress the social–emotional and behavioral aspects of school success, including such areas as bullying prevention, character education, social–emotional learning, and schoolwide behavioral support (CASEL, 2003; Cooper, 2008).

Given limited resources and intense scrutiny, educators are faced with difficult and important decisions about investments in educational programs; therefore, high-quality information about which programs have the strongest evidence of positive impact is critical. Although the definitions of "effective" or "evidence-based" programming, as well as "scientific rigor," have been the subject of fervent debate (National Research Council, 2005), schools and districts are guided by national policy toward programs tested with *randomized controlled trials* in which participants are randomly assigned to an intervention group (or groups) and a control (or comparison) condition to examine the impact of a program on a set of outcomes (see Brass et al., 2006). The Institute of Education Sciences prioritizes the use of randomized experiments to determine causal relationships, as demonstrated in the *What Works Clearinghouse,* a U.S.

Department of Education (2005) guide for school and district administrators of educational programs with evidence of effectiveness from randomized trials. The U.S. Department of Education published a final priority in which randomized trials to assess program and curricular effectiveness were highlighted (see Brass et al., 2006).

However, even those who believe that randomization is the gold standard in education research recognize that it is difficult to conduct a high-quality randomized controlled trial. Discussion of how to design and implement a randomized trial has focused on the enhancement of methodological rigor in large-scale research (see Raudenbush, 1997), but less attention has been paid to the ethical and practical considerations driving the decisions of education researchers working on a smaller scale. In this chapter, we respond to the gap by focusing on the design of not only *rigorous* but also *responsive* and *responsible* intervention studies to promote academic learning and support the social and behavioral components of students' success in school. By rigorous, we mean methodologically sound, such that the data allow estimation of program impact on outcomes of interest, for which groups, and under what conditions. By responsive, we mean the systematic incorporation of the perspectives of key stakeholders in the intervention research process, including school staff, community collaborators, and families. And, by responsible, we mean ethically aware, logistically reasonable, and educationally meaningful. The overall aim is to assist educational researchers to design studies that produce relevant and rigorous information on the best methods for developing students in schools.

OVERARCHING DESIGN DECISIONS IN CAUSAL ANALYSES

One of the main tenets of research methods is the interdependent and reciprocal relationship among (a) the research questions, (b) the design used to answer those questions, and (c) the conclusions one can draw on the basis of the findings. In the case of intervention research in schools, the ultimate research question involves the issue of *causality*, or whether implementation of the intervention caused change in particular outcomes of interest.[1] Although there has been considerable debate on the nature of causal inference and the best way to enhance it, experimental manipulation of the intervention condition is generally seen as the most appropriate research design for causal analyses. However, sometimes it is not possible to randomize subjects to groups, and often it is necessary and interesting to answer questions beyond the main question of causal impact. In the following sections, we discuss when to use experimental and quasi-experimental designs to study school-based programs, and the strengths and challenges of each approach. We focus on experimental studies because of their ability to answer causal questions, with particular attention to issues of randomization, statistical power, control groups, and logic models to guide outcome, cost, and fidelity assessment.

Decision Points in Research Design: Experimental Versus Quasi-Experimental Designs

Policymakers and educators are acutely interested in which programs help students succeed in school and gain knowledge and skills to contribute productively to society. Thus, the question of causality—which programs affect the key outcomes of interest—is the ultimate question that must be addressed. Although use of randomized trials is generally seen as the best way to answer this question, this design can be costly in terms of material and personnel resources. Because of the resource demands, methodologists often advocate for establishing preliminary evidence of intervention impact prior to implementing a randomized trial (e.g., Biglan, Ary, & Wagenaar, 2000). At the same time, alternative research designs, such as quasi-experimental studies, may be more flexible than experimental designs in their ability to address questions related to feasibility and implementation. In some cases, random assignment is logistically unfeasible or imprudent because of potential negative impact on the relationship between school officials and the researchers; in these cases, alternative methods should be explored.

---

[1] For a discussion of the philosophical debate around the nature of and ability to detect causal relationships, see White (1990). A sampling of writing on the methodological debate includes Cook (2002); Bhattacharjee (2005); and Concato, Shah, and Horwitz (2000).

Therefore, the decision regarding whether to use an experimental design is related to the primary research questions for the particular stage of intervention development, as well as considerations relevant to the community in which the intervention is being examined. For example, when the interventions or curricula are in the initial stage of development, or alternatively, major adaptations are taking place, it may be important to assess whether the intervention is feasible to implement, how to best implement it, whether further modifications are needed, and what preliminary evidence of impact is available. Likewise, when schools or communities have, as their priority, issues of feasibility and implementation, or instead have strong concerns about randomization as a method, a quasi-experimental approach in which matched controls are used to estimate initial impact may be most appropriate.

Quasi-Experimental Designs: Strengths and Limitations

Although quasi-experimental designs do not use randomization to groups, high-quality quasi-experiments share many of the characteristics of randomized designs, including measurement of outcomes, implementation of the intervention, and sampling of participants (Cook & Campbell, 1979). This methodological rigor improves the *external validity* of the design, or the ability of a program to be implemented across different settings with different populations and deliver the same outcomes. In well-controlled quasi-experiments, participants, classrooms, or schools may be assigned by means such as self-selection or convenience, such as when particular schools have volunteered to try a new program. Researchers are then in the position to decide on comparison groups to match intervention participants or schools on a set of criteria (i.e., school or class size, student background, or test scores). Like experimental studies, quasi-experimental designs in school settings also may involve group or cluster designs, where the level of comparison is the group (e.g., classroom, school) rather than the individual student. Unlike experimental studies, however, the groups of clusters in quasi-experimental designs are assigned to conditions (such as use of particular instructional methods or prevention program) in a nonrandom way.

The main drawback of nonrandomized designs is the threat to *internal validity*, or the confidence with which the impact can be attributed to the intervention being studied (Cook & Campbell, 1979). This can be enhanced in a quasi-experimental study by careful matching of comparison with intervention groups. For example, if the study is designed to examine the presence of teacher aides in high school science classrooms, and randomization may have serious negative consequences on the researcher–school relationship, matching by classroom should include attention to relevant variables such as class size and composition, teacher training and quality, or other characteristics that might interact with intervention effects. Causal inferences can be made with greater confidence when creating matched groups based on propensity scores—the aggregate of relevant covariates that predicts the probability of a particular group receiving an intervention. However, even with strongly matched conditions, it is more of a risk in quasi-experimental studies that some unmeasured feature is responsible for the perceived outcomes (Shadish, Cook, & Campbell, 2002). Thus, the use of quasi-experimental designs requires special care in the interpretation of the data, as the lack of random assignment makes it more difficult to draw causal conclusions with confidence.

EXPERIMENTAL DESIGNS: RANDOMIZATION AND CONTROL GROUPS

When there is true randomness in assignment, randomization allows causal inferences to be made about the relationship between implementation of a program and subsequent outcomes (e.g., Multisite Violence Prevention Project, 2004). However, there are several critical decision points in randomized controlled trials that play a role in enhancing the validity of the causal inferences. As with quasi-experimental trials, one of the first decisions involves the nature of the research questions of interest. If a randomized trial is used, it is likely that the intervention is well developed and there has been some early examination of its feasibility or impact. Experimental approaches can answer the question of program impact on the relevant outcomes but also can assess more complex and multilayered questions (St. Pierre & Rossi, 2006). For example, researchers may be interested in examining whether one method has a stronger impact than another, or whether one program works better for certain students under certain conditions. Thus, the basic question of impact may be enhanced by multi-layered and multi-informant research designs to determine not only what works but also how it works and for whom.

Level of Randomization: Student, Classroom, or School

Another major decision point related to the intervention being examined and research questions being asked is the level at which to randomize. Most commonly, researchers randomly assign students, classrooms, or schools to intervention and control conditions. When students are the level of randomization, it is easier to recruit more participants and thus have greater statistical power to detect differences across subgroups (i.e., low-achieving students, externalizing students). When examining programs targeting individual skills and nonclassroom settings, it may be possible to randomize at the level of the child. The level used for randomization affects the level at which generalizations can be made about program impact. For example, randomizing by individual child would allow conclusions about program impact on child-level outcomes, such as individual skills or abilities. However, this would preclude an examination of the ecologic changes related to classroom or school functioning. Therefore, such design decisions must be made with an eye toward the hypothesized nature of program impacts and structure. Randomizing children to groups also presents a challenge given that much of what occurs during the school day occurs in classrooms, which are assigned in a nonrandom manner. In addition, there is the likelihood of *diffusion-of-treatment* effects (see Aiken & West, 1990) in which individuals randomly assigned to one condition influence individuals not assigned to the condition.

These diffusion-of-treatment effects can occur when randomizing at the teacher or classroom level as well. For example, teachers trained in a novel instructional strategy may discuss or share aspects of their training with colleagues at the same school, which has been called "passing it on" (see McCall & Green, 2004, p. 7). However, when the "treatment" being studied cannot be easily transmitted, such as examining the impact of access to classroom computers or involvement of peer reading tutors in classroom instruction, random assignment of classroom clusters can be considered. It allows examination of critical classroom-level outcomes, such as mean achievement, teacher practices, and classroom climate, and it is significantly less resource intensive than school-level randomization. However, ethical and practical considerations are particularly acute for teachers when considering random assignment at the classroom level. For example, teachers randomly chosen for computer access or cross-age tutoring may feel uncomfortable accepting the additional resources; alternatively, experimental teachers may resent the extra time it takes to adjust their instruction to a new program or set of resources. Even if teachers are inclined to participate, the potential for negativity may be enough to preclude researchers from choosing this design. At the least, researchers who choose the classroom as the randomization unit must find creative and powerful ways of addressing these issues prior to launching the study to avoid potential damage to collegiality or school climate.

Cluster randomization at the school level reduces the likelihood of treatment diffusion from intervention to control conditions, allows measurement of changes in the school as a system, and offers the opportunity to examine variations among schools (see Multisite Violence Prevention Project, 2004). Given the need to recruit and maintain sufficient numbers of schools to detect effects, it is the most logistically difficult and resource-intensive level of randomization. Beyond practical barriers, ethical concerns may arise when asking control schools to refrain from implementing promising programs. Even when researchers are able to overcome these practical and ethical issues to randomize at level of the school, it is not uncommon in longitudinal intervention studies for other factors to interfere with the randomized design over time (e.g., non-random attrition).

However, because of the policy priority to improve the quality of U.S. schools and the wide variability across schools in climate and functioning, and therefore need to study schools as systems, it is important to address these practical and ethical barriers. Recently, researchers have made progress in creatively solving these problems. For example, in the field trial of Success for All, Borman and colleagues (Borman et al., 2005a, 2005b) randomly assigned schools to implement the reading curriculum either in Grades K to 2, with Grades 3 to 5 serving as comparison grades, or in Grades 3 to 5, with Grades K to 2 serving as comparison grades. Thus, schools served as both intervention and comparison groups. Other approaches involve random assignment of schools to implement one of two or more interventions, such that no treatment-as-usual comparison group is used or random assignment of matched pairs such that if one school withdraws from the study, the partner school is removed from analyses in order to preserve the randomized design.

Appropriate Control Groups

Another major decision point in randomized trials concerns the selection of comparison or control conditions. Having a control condition permits researchers' understanding of what would have happened had the intervention not been delivered. Therefore, in the simplest design, the control clusters are assigned the *treatment-as-usual* condition. This increases external validity while simultaneously making the implementation of the randomized trials more feasible in schools, because it may be unethical to impose restrictions on control schools and impractical to implement an alternative intervention as a comparison. One challenge with treatment-as-usual controls is that participants in the control clusters, after they learn their assignment, may adopt programs similar to the one being studied, and thus reduce the ability to detect a causal impact. Even if no new programs are adopted, control students and teachers are getting "treatment" in schools, thus it is critical for researchers to collect data that indicate the kinds of resources, programs, and curricula available to the control group to consider these in analyses of intervention impact.

At times, researcher- or community-driven ethical concerns supersede the consideration of a treatment-as-usual control group. For example, teachers, principals, or districts may not be willing to participate without all participants receiving the potential benefit of the program. One alternative to the treatment-as-usual control is a *waitlist* control in which clusters assigned to the control condition receive the intervention after a specified time. Because the program is eventually implemented in these groups, the ethical issue is mitigated. This approach also mirrors the strategies school districts often use in implementing novel programs or curricula. When facing challenges of limited resources, school districts frequently "roll out" programs gradually. Researchers working in partnership with district representatives can capitalize on the ecological validity of the waitlist control approach by using random assignment to select how schools follow the implementation timeline. The main drawback, besides the need for the additional resources to implement the program in the control clusters, is reduced ability to analyze differences between the intervention and control groups that may appear only over time.

Other designs guided by strong theory involve the control clusters receiving a particular type of treatment from the start: This may include a component of the program, a different program targeting the same outcomes, or a different program targeting different outcomes. For example, Ialongo, Poduska, Werthamer, and Kellam (2001) compared programs that used different mechanisms (classrooms vs. families) to target risk for conduct problems. Cappella and Weinstein (2006) compared two programs similar in structure but different in content and target outcomes (social conflict resolution vs. reading achievement). In these and related designs, experimental and control participants all receive a program designed to have an impact on meaningful outcomes and answer research questions beyond the question of causal impact. The difficulty arises in interpreting causal impact in a design without a no-treatment control group and may speak to the importance of embedding these studies in a larger program of research. Thus, once clearly interpretable positive impacts are documented for a particular program, subsequent evaluations can use differently defined comparison groups.

Maximizing Statistical Power

After making the critical decisions about research questions, level of randomization, and control groups, investigators need to attend to methods for maximizing statistical power in quantitatively oriented, cluster-randomized designs. Without adequate *statistical power,* or ability to know when a significant effect is present, the research design is insufficient to adequately address the research questions at hand. The emphasis in cluster-randomized designs is on the number of *clusters* (e.g., classrooms or schools) rather than the number of *participants* (e.g., students) in each cluster (Blair & Higgins, 1985). In these considerations, investigators must address the relative cost of sampling more clusters as well as more participants per cluster.[2] For example, in a school-based intervention study, recruiting each additional school and ensuring that school's continued commitment to the intervention throughout the duration of the study is far more expensive than sampling a greater number of students within each school. To maximize statistical power in cluster-randomized designs, researchers can use efficient experimental designs and analytical approaches. One common approach is to *block clusters* prior to randomization. This involves matching schools or classrooms on relevant variables and conducting random assignment within those matched blocks, such as school size or percentage of students in the free lunch program (Raudenbush, Martinez, & Spybrook, 2007), to minimize potential differences between intervention and control conditions. A second approach to maximizing statistical power is to *adjust for covariates,* which means to statistically control for a theoretically and empirically derived covariate that is measured prior to intervention implementation (e.g., baseline reading scores). Bloom and colleagues demonstrated how controlling for baseline covariates—pretest assessments, in particular—increases power in group-randomized designs such that substantially lower numbers of groups are needed to detect program impacts (Bloom, Richburg-Hayes, & Black, 2007). Furthermore, findings suggest that school-level pretests may be as effective in maximizing precision as student-level pretests, which are typically much more expensive and resource-intensive to obtain. Both of these strategies—blocking and using covariates—can maximize statistical power to detect significant program impacts in group-randomized designs.

---

[2] For a full description and discussion of considerations of sampling clusters and participants within clusters, see Raudenbush (1997).

MEASUREMENT ISSUES ACROSS LEVELS, METHODS, AND INFORMANTS

As these design decisions are being made, school-based intervention researchers must develop a plan for (a) implementing the intervention trial, (b) measuring implementation quality, (c) measuring intervention outcomes, and (d) understanding intervention processes.

Logic Models as a Guide for Assessment

A *logic model* or *causal model* provides a theoretically and empirically driven roadmap of the study design that guides the researcher in implementation, assessment, and data analyses (Weiss, 1995). Logic models reflect representations of the relationships among the components, including a "plausible, sensible model of how a program is supposed to work" (Bickman, 1987, p. 5; see Figure 3.1 for an example). In general, logic models provide a structure for determining when and what to measure so that resources are used effectively and efficiently to maximize the chance of detecting an impact if one exists. In particular, logic models include information about the structure and content of the intervention, the targets or mechanisms through which the intervention will work, and the meaningful proximal and distal outcomes.

Of particular importance in group-randomized designs, the logic model can depict both the child-level context—such as information about what the children receive in terms of curriculum and what the children take away in terms of skills and knowledge—and the classroom- or school-level context. For example, if one of the main activities in the intervention involves training elementary school teachers to use a particular math curriculum, the logic model provides information about where and how teachers are trained, what skills and information the teachers are provided, and which teacher-level outcomes are proposed (i.e., change in knowledge, attitudes, sense of efficacy). Likewise, if randomizing by school clusters, relevant school-level variables, such as school climate, can be assessed to determine whether changes in those variables result from participation in a unified curriculum. Evaluations of interventions such as Cook's studies

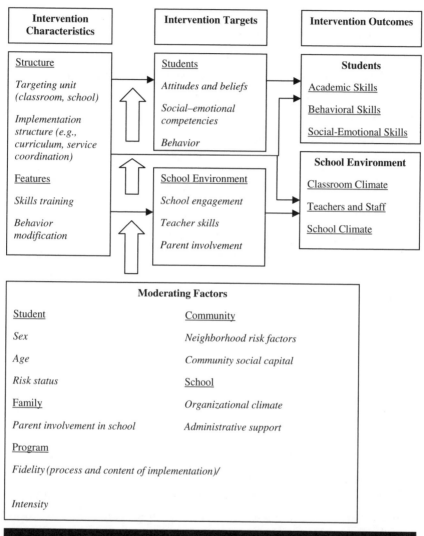

Figure 3.1

Sample logic model structure for school-based intervention research design.

of James Comer's whole-school reform programs (Cook et al., 1999; Cook, Murphy, & Hunt, 2000) have demonstrated the importance of measuring multiple levels of school contexts. Comer's School Development Program (SDP; Comer, Haynes, Joyner, & Ben Avie, 1996) is a school-level intervention that specifies processes and structures that enable schools to develop and monitor educational and social goals as a means toward increasing student achievement. In a cluster randomized design, Cook et al. (1999) reported that the Comer project had an impact on student academic scores, as well as school social climate, teacher self-efficacy, and student social behavior. Thus, use of these designs allows researchers to evaluate the impact of an intervention on place, such as classrooms or schools, as well as the impact on individuals.

Outcome Assessment

Once an adequate logic model has been laid out, an assessment strategy can be developed that maps onto key characteristics of the model. This strategy must consider three areas: (a) timing of assessment, (b) method or source of assessment, and (c) level of outcome assessed. We address each of these in turn.

In terms of timing, outcome assessments must include pretest measures that take place prior to intervention implementation, as well as posttest assessments at the times at which change is expected to occur. *Proximal* outcomes, or the specific outcomes expected immediately following implementation, are measured shortly after the active intervention has been completed. *Distal* outcomes, or more global impacts that are expected over time, are measured after a theoretically meaningful amount of time has passed. Take, for example, a school-based, family-focused program providing knowledge, empowerment, and opportunity to build productive home–school relationships. Baseline measures are gathered on both proximal and distal outcomes prior to intervention implementation. Shortly after the end of the program, proximal outcomes related to parent knowledge, attitudes, and beliefs may be measured. After specific opportunities to participate in the life of the classroom or school, researchers can assess family behavioral outcomes, such as attendance at parent–teacher conferences, involvement in homework, or participation in home-school notes. The distal outcomes related to student motivation, academic engagement, and achievement can be assessed after sufficient time has passed for parent behaviors to affect students. Throughout, key moderating variables must be assessed (see

Figure 3.1), including covariates that will be used to adjust intervention impact estimates.[3]

Decisions about the method or source of assessment vary depending on the outcome being assessed as well as the characteristics of the reporters. Particular individuals may be the most accurate reporters for particular outcomes. For example, internalizing symptoms can be assessed with self-report, teacher practices can be observed using a standardized system (see chap. 4, this volume), and child social behaviors can be accurately measured by peer report. In some cases, using multiple reporters can yield more complete information about complex constructs. For example, parents and teachers may complete surveys on student work habits for a snapshot of student productivity in the home and the classroom. Researchers may assess school climate with a heterogeneous group of reporters—students, teachers, and administrators—to reflect the complex nature of the construct. In the end, systematic consideration of the age, education, and language abilities of the reporters produces the most precise and accurate measurement.

Finally, in randomized trials of school interventions, the vehicles for change and the targets of outcomes may be embedded at multiple levels (Multisite Violence Prevention Project, 2004). Curricula may be intended to produce changes in individual students as well as designed to target classroom or school functioning. Likewise, the mechanisms for producing change differ from traditional laboratory- or clinic-based intervention research in that the "intervention agents" are often teachers or school staff. Therefore, the interventions must involve an intermediary step to train the intervention agents (e.g., teachers) to implement the intervention components. This step can introduce risks in drawing conclusions. For example, if an intervention does not produce significant impacts in a randomized trial, the implication could be either that the intervention is not effective or that implementation of the intervention was not implemented as intended. Raudenbush (2003) described a distinction between *theory failure,* which refers to the instance when a program is implemented as intended but the impact is not as hypothesized, and *implementation failure,*

---

[3] See Petrosino (2000) for a discussion of mediators and moderators in evaluation of child-focused intervention.

which refers to situations in which a program was not implemented as intended. This distinction is a critical one, and it highlights the importance of addressing all levels of implementation for measurement of both fidelity and outcomes.

Fidelity Measurement

Fidelity of *program implementation* (Moncher & Prinz, 1991), also referred to as *treatment integrity* (e.g., Dane & Schneider, 1998) or *implementation quality* (Domitrovich & Greenberg, 2000), has been defined as the "degree to which treatment is delivered as intended" (Yeaton & Sechrest, 1981, p. 160). Assessing fidelity of program implementation is a critical element of an evaluation, particularly in light of data demonstrating that variability in the quality of implementation is related to program outcomes (e.g., Botvin, Baker, Dusenbury, Botvin, & Diaz, 1995). If a program is not implemented with fidelity to the theoretical model and program benchmarks, the effectiveness of the program cannot be adequately judged. In the event of null findings, assessment of fidelity can help the research team distinguish failure of program theory from implementation failure (Dobson & Cook, 1980). Although the study of implementation is in its infancy, specific strategies have been promoted to help one understand the degree to which programs are implemented as intended, the quality of implementation, and individuals' attitudes toward implementation (Domitrovich & Greenberg, 2000). Utilizing implementation information may not only help evaluators in their interpretation of evaluation findings but also inform interventionists in their quest for program improvement. A full discussion of implementation measurement approaches is included in chapter 6 of this volume. In the upcoming section, we include a brief discussion of how to measure implementation fidelity in the context of experimental and quasi-experimental designs.

The principal strategy of fidelity measurement should be to rely on the logic model to provide the specific program components and active ingredients of the intervention (Durlak, 1998), as this will yield a starting point for laying out a comprehensive fidelity measurement plan. One school-based intervention project in which one of the authors (Greta Massetti) has been involved as coprincipal investigator was a multisite evaluation of seven programs targeting social and character development (Pelham, Massetti, & Waschbusch, 2007). For this study, a fidelity model was developed that characterized program elements across sites based on the intended agents and targets of the program. For each site, fidelity models identified intervention components provided to (a) teachers (e.g., training); (b) students by teachers (e.g., curriculum); (c) parents (e.g., meetings); and (d) all members of the school (e.g., expectations and rules). Because teachers may vary on the amount of the program they implement (fidelity content) and the integrity of that implementation (fidelity process), both implementation process and content were measured for all program components.

The sample fidelity plan from one site depicts the model for four of the components of the comprehensive intervention program (see Table 3.1; Massetti, Waschbusch, & Pelham, 2006). The model illustrates how the program components were divided based on the targets of service delivery (e.g., teachers, students); in addition, measurements of content and process were developed to assess specific characteristics of each component. For several components, more than one indicator was collected to reflect the complete implementation picture. For example, to determine the extent to which the teacher training component was implemented with fidelity, investigators tracked both the number of teachers who completed all training modules and the number of hours of training each teacher completed. For some indicators, new assessment methods were developed, such as a novel classroom observation scheme to capture the particular strategies covered in the intervention program. For others, archival information was collected, such as teacher training attendance rosters. Owing to concerns about the validity of teacher reports, researchers relied on external and more objective measures of implementation (e.g., Massetti, Pelham, & Waschbusch, 2007).

Formative Research in the Context of Randomized Controlled Trials

Related to fidelity measurement is the opportunity to collect formative data within a randomized trial to provide a deeper understanding of the

Table 3.1
Sample Fidelity Measurement Model for Randomized Trials of School-Based Programs

Services delivered to	Service provided	Program component	Content indicator	Process indicator
Teachers	Teacher training in classroom and behavior management	Teacher training	Percentage of teachers completing full training modules; number of training hours per teacher	Training evaluation ratings completed by supervisor
	Consultation services	Teacher consultation	Percentage of intended consultation visits completed	Consultant evaluation ratings completed by supervisor, teachers
Students by teachers	Classroom management program, schoolwide positive behavioral support strategies	Classroom management	Components present during classroom observations; consultant implementation ratings	Evaluation ratings completed by consultants; classroom observation ratings
Students by schools	After-school skills training program for identified children	After-school program	Percentage of sessions held; content covered during sessions	Program evaluation ratings completed by supervisor

contexts in which the intervention is being implemented and the individuals involved in the implementation (e.g., Ostrom, Lerner, & Freel, 1995; Petrosino, 2000). The goal is to produce relevant, precise, and efficient research toward the development of educational methods and programs that continue to advance both science and practice.

Formative research methods are particularly useful during two phases of the intervention research: (a) early in the process of adapting programs and determining research designs for diverse school settings, and (b) later in the process of implementing or coordinating programs in innovative ways (Lipsey & Cordray, 2000). Multiple forms of data collected from diverse perspectives during the earlier stages can be immediately integrated into the ongoing study to help guide decisions. Toward this end, systematic, iterative, and short-term designs with straightforward analyses are most useful for feeding information back in a timely manner. Gathering data from multiple sources across the school (i.e., students, parents, teachers, other personnel) may be important as investigators consider the varied viewpoint of individuals whose involvement is critical to program success (Conduct Problems Prevention Research Group, 2002; Connor-Smith & Weisz, 2003). Beyond program adaptation, these multi-informant formative methods can help investigators develop research methods that are meaningful to the population and setting studied (Israel et al., 1995; Nastasi, 2004).

One randomized intervention study in high-poverty Chicago schools utilized formative methods to inform the study of a model, Links to Learning, to support teachers and parents in promoting learning among children with disruptive behavior problems (Atkins, Frazier, & Cappella, 2006). Early in the research process, investigators collected formative data with community mental health leaders and parent advocates, whose input led to a decision to randomize schools to condition after limiting the pool of schools to a minimal distance from cooperating agencies to facilitate transportation to services for control group families. Interviews with educational and agency administrators provided clarification on the structure of school and mental health records, enabling the development of precise and efficient measurement of student achievement, attendance, disciplinary referrals, and mental health services to serve as covariates in outcome analyses. Thus, formative data led to research design and measurement decisions that enhanced the likelihood that the study would accurately test the ability of the intervention model to promote student learning and positive behavior (Cappella & Atkins, 2006).

Formative data collected later during the intervention research process are useful for interpreting or explaining experimental findings of program impact as well as for informing the subsequent wave of program dissemination and evaluation (Gittelsohn et al., 2006). During these stages, mixed-method approaches may best facilitate breadth and depth of understanding of experimental findings (Greene & Caracelli, 1997). For example, qualitative methods may help one to understand why an educational model is not being implemented to fidelity or how the model is being used, whereas quantitative methods may be useful in assessing what is being implemented and who is doing so.

ETHICAL ISSUES IN INTERVENTION RESEARCH

Infusing every design and data decision are ethical concerns. University, school district, and community agency research boards are designed to keep participant interests at the fore. However, beyond oversight by research boards, school-based researchers conducting randomized trials are responsible for (a) including multiple voices in design and measurement decisions, (b) considering the research burden on participants, and (c) attending to possible iatrogenic effects.

Inclusion of Multiple Voices

When cocreated by researchers and community members, randomized designs become more ethically sound and community relevant. Researchers can use strategies such as resource mapping or asset maps to learn which individuals and organizations are influential in the school community, and then key stakeholders can be invited to participate in the research planning (Ostrom et al., 1995). These community meetings are not an opportunity for researchers to persuade community members about the appropriateness of a particular design but a chance to engage in conversation about the best method for studying the impact of a particular program. Dialogue may lead to more realistic and thoughtful decisions about research questions, control groups, timing of assessments, and sources of measurement.

As an example, in one project in which one of the authors (Elise Cappella) was the primary investigator (Cappella & Weinstein, 2006), the original plan to include a business-as-usual control group was replaced after discussion with elementary school principals. Instead, the control group was assigned a comparison "Reading Club" intervention that matched the social problem-solving program in structure and time but differed in content and target outcomes. This change in research design led to the ability to test research questions of importance to both the researchers and the educators around the specificity of effects and the mechanisms of change. The timing of assessments can be strengthened by participant input as well, particularly in the areas of maximizing construct validity and minimizing missing data. Finally, dialogue during research planning may produce information from school personnel whose perspectives would not automatically be assessed but who may offer important information that adds to the assessment of a particular construct (see chap. 1, this volume).

Measurement Burden on Participants

Although comprehensive and multi-informant assessment produces the best evidence of the impact of an intervention on outcomes (e.g., Ogles & Owens, 2004), it is equally important to consider the measurement burden on research participants (as well as implementation burden on intervention staff). To conduct both rigorous and responsible intervention research is to assess the critical outcomes accurately and efficiently without undue encumbrance on participants and accompanying reductions in data quality, a particular challenge when there are multiple and complex outcomes to assess. Whenever possible, researchers must create priority lists of outcomes, with the primary constructs assessed with the greatest precision and secondary constructs assessed more globally. Measures that have good internal reliability and construct validity, as well as the most informed reporters, should be chosen for each outcome. Creative methods also can be used to lessen measurement burden in multiple time point, longitudinal designs without significant reductions in the power. One such method is assessing a random subsample of participants in each cluster at each time point so that every participant has multiple assessments but no participant is assessed every time.

Potential Iatrogenic Effects

A final and critical aspect of school intervention research design is creating a system for early recognition of potential negative intervention impacts. When "do no harm" is the primary foundation of responsible research, investigators need a method by which all research staff know when harm is being done, or alternatively, when the intervention fails to deliver and student needs are largely unmet. As an example, in the National Institute of Mental Health Collaborative Multimodal Treatment Study, a multisite randomized trial of treatment of children with attention-deficit/hyperactivity disorder, an emergency/adjunct services manual was created with clear steps in the case of emergencies or threats to implementation (Abikoff et al., 2002). Although most school programs and educational curricula are unlikely to have severe negative consequences, researchers are responsible for having an explicit plan for when and how to alter the intervention and research protocols when participants are threatened. In the case of potential iatrogenic impacts, the purity of the research design comes second.

CONCLUSION: RIGOROUS, RESPONSIVE, AND RESPONSIBLE RESEARCH DESIGN

The past decade has brought attention to schooling—its nature and its consequences. Educators and policymakers in the United States are looking for guidance, and researchers are in a position to provide it. With the opportunity to guide the educational community to work effectively with diverse students comes the responsibility to produce accurate, efficient, and relevant information about what methods and programs are effective for which groups of children in which settings. Methodological rigor in school intervention research design is critical. Decisions related to the type of design to answer the research questions, the formation and treatment of control groups, the creation of a coherent and concise logic model, and the development of appropriate assessment methods all contribute to the ability to interpret findings with confidence and precision. Equally critical is community responsiveness at each step. Educational researchers must build into their decision making an awareness of and openness to the specific community in which the randomized trial is taking place, as well as the broader community that will apply the research in practice and policy. This includes incorporating multiple perspectives into the research design, using formative research to better understand the contexts and individuals involved, and maintaining participant well-being at every step. Without rigorous research, the findings are difficult to interpret. Without responsive research, the findings may not be meaningful. With both, researchers can help guide schools toward methods and programs that make a positive difference in the lives of children.

REFERENCES

Abikoff, H., Arnold, L. E., Newcorn, J. H., Elliott, G. R., Hechtman, L., Severe, J. B., et al. (2002). Emergency/adjunct services and attrition prevention for randomized clinical trials in children: The MTA manual-based solution. *Journal of the American Academy of Child & Adolescent Psychiatry, 41,* 498–504.

Aiken, L. S., & West, S. G. (1990). Invalidity of true experiments: Self-report pretest biases. *Evaluation Review, 14,* 374–390.

Atkins, M. S., Frazier, S. L., & Cappella, E. (2006, June). *Mental health service model for children in high poverty urban schools: Uniting indigenous resources around learning.* Paper presented at the annual meeting of the American Psychological Society, New York, NY.

Bhattacharjee, Y. (2005, March). Can randomized trials answer the question of what works? *Science, 307,* 1861–1863.

Bickman, L. (Ed.). (1987). *Using program theory in evaluation.* San Francisco: Jossey-Bass.

Biglan, A., Ary, D., & Wagenaar, A. C. (2000). The value of interrupted time-series experiments for community intervention research. *Prevention Science, 1,* 31–49.

Blair, R. C., & Higgins, J. (1985). A comparison of the power of the paired samples rank transform statistic to that of Wilcoxon's signed ranks statistic. *Journal of Educational Statistics, 10,* 368–383.

Bloom, H. S., Richburg-Hayes, L., & Black, A. R. (2007). Using covariates to improve precision for studies that randomize schools to evaluate educational interventions. *Educational Evaluation and Policy Analysis, 29,* 30–59.

Borman, G., Slavin, R. E., Cheung, A., Chamberlain, A., Madden, N. A., & Chambers, B. (2005a). The national randomized field trial of Success for All: Second-year outcomes. *American Educational Research Journal, 42,* 673–696.

Borman, G., Slavin, R. E., Cheung, A., Chamberlain, A., Madden, N. A., & Chambers, B. (2005b). Success for All: First-year results from the national randomized field trial. *Educational Evaluation and Policy Analysis, 27,* 1–22.

Botvin, G. J., Baker, E., Dusenbury, L., Botvin, E. M., & Diaz, T. (1995). Long-term follow-up results of a randomized drug abuse prevention trial in a White middle-class population. *JAMA, 273,* 1106–1112.

Brass, C. T., Nunez-Neto, B., & Williams, E. D. (2006). *Congress and program evaluation: An overview of randomized controlled trials (RCTs) and related issues.* Washington, DC: Congressional Research Service.

Cappella, E., & Atkins, M. S. (2006, April). *Links to Learning: Stage I. Formative research to develop an accessible, effective, and sustainable mental health model for children in urban poor schools.* Poster session presented at the annual meeting of the American Educational Research Association, San Francisco, CA.

Cappella, E., & Weinstein, R. S. (2006). The prevention of social aggression among girls. *Social Development, 15,* 434–462.

CASEL. (2003). *Safe and sound: An educational leader's guide to evidence-based SEL programs.* Chicago: CASEL, University of Illinois, Department of Psychology.

Comer, J. P., Haynes, N. M., Joyner, E. T., & Ben Avie, M. (1996). *Rallying the whole village: The Comer process for reforming education.* New York: Teachers College Press.

Concato, J., Shah, N., & Horwitz, R. I. (2000). Randomized, controlled trials, observational studies, and the hierarchy of research designs. *New England Journal of Medicine, 342,* 1887–1892.

Conduct Problems Prevention Group. (2002). The implementation of the fast track program: An example of large-scale prevention science efficacy trial. *Journal of Abnormal Child Psychology, 30,* 1–17.

Connor-Smith, J. K., & Weisz, J. R. (2003). Applying treatment outcome research in clinical practice: Techniques for adapting interventions to the real world. *Child and Adolescent Mental Health, 8,* 3–10.

Cook, T. D. (2002). Randomized experiments in educational policy research: A critical examination of the reasons the educational evaluation community has offered for not doing them. *Educational Evaluation and Policy Analysis, 24,* 175–199.

Cook, T., & Campbell, D. (1979). *Quasi-experimentation.* New York: Rand McNally.

Cook, T., Habib, F., Phillips, M., Settersten, R., Shagle, S., & Degirmencioglu, S. (1999). Comer's school development program in Prince George's County, Maryland: A theory-based evaluation. *American Educational Research Journal, 36,* 543–597.

Cook, T. D., Murphy, R. F., & Hunt, H. D. (2000). Comer's school development program in Chicago: A theory-based evaluation. *American Educational Research Journal, 37,* 535–597.

Cooper, J. L. (2008). The federal case for school-based mental health services and supports. *Journal of the American Academy of Child and Adolescent Psychiatry, 47,* 4–8.

Dane, A. V., & Schneider, B. H. (1998). Program integrity in primary and early secondary prevention: Are implementation effects out of control? *Clinical Psychology Review, 18,* 23–45.

Dobson, D., & Cook, T. J. (1980). Avoiding Type III error in program evaluation: Results from a field experiment. *Evaluation and Program Planning, 3,* 269–276.

Domitrovich, C. E., & Greenberg, M. T. (2000). The study of implementation: Current findings from effective programs that prevent mental disorders in school-aged children. *Journal of Educational and Psychological Consultation, 11,* 193–221.

Durlak, J. A. (1998). Why program implementation is important. *Journal of Prevention and Intervention in the Community, 17,* 5–18.

Eisenhart, M., & Towne, L. (2003). Contestation and change in national policy on "scientifically based" education research. *Educational Researcher, 32,* 31–38.

Federal Interagency Forum on Child and Family Statistics. (2007). *America's children: Key national indicators of well-being, 2007.* Washington, DC: U.S. Government Printing Office.

Gittelsohn, J., Steckler, A., Johnson, C. C., Pratt, C., Grieser, M., Pickrel, J., et al. (2006). Formative research in school and community-based health programs and studies: "State of the art" and the TAAG approach. *Health Education and Behavior, 33,* 25–39.

Greene, J. C., & Caracelli, V. J. (1997). Defining and describing the paradigm issue in mixed-method evaluation. In J. C. Greene & V. J. Caracelli (Eds.), *Advances in mixed-method evaluation: The challenges and benefits of integrating diverse paradigms* (pp. 5–17). San Francisco: Jossey-Bass.

Ialongo, N., Poduska, J., Werthamer, L., & Kellam, S. (2001). The distal impact of two first-grade preventive interventions on conduct problems and disorder in early adolescence. *Journal of Emotional and Behavioral Disorders, 9,* 146–160.

Israel, B. A., Cummings, K. M., Dignan, M. B., Heaney, C. A, Perales, D. P., Simons-Morton, B. G., & Zimmerman, M. A. (1995). Evaluation of health education programs: Current assessment and future directions. *Health Education Quarterly, 22,* 364–389.

Lipsey, M. W., & Cordray, D. S. (2000). Evaluation methods for social intervention. *Annual Review of Psychology, 51,* 345–375.

Massetti, G. M., Pelham, W. E., & Waschbusch, D. A. (2007, June). *Teacher fidelity of use of behavior management strategies: Relationships among observations, self-report, and children's disruptive behavior.* Poster session presented at the annual meeting of the Institute of Education Sciences Research Conference, Washington, DC.

Massetti, G. M., Waschbusch, D. A., & Pelham, W. E. (2006, May). Use of behavior management strategies by teachers: Fidelity and implementation of the ABC program. In T. Haegerich (Chair), *The social and character development randomized trial: Assessing intervention fidelity and traditional practice in "control" conditions.* Symposium conducted at the meeting of the Society for Prevention Research, San Antonio, TX.

McCall, R. B., & Green, B. L. (2004). Beyond the methodological gold standards of behavioral research: Considerations for practice and policy. *Social Policy Report, 18,* 3–19.

Moncher, F. J., & Prinz, R. J. (1991). Treatment fidelity in outcome studies. *Clinical Psychology Review, 11,* 247–266.

Multisite Violence Prevention Project. (2004). Lessons learned in the Multisite Violence Prevention Project collaboration: Big questions require large efforts. *American Journal of Preventive Medicine, 26,* 62–71.

Nastasi, B. K. (2004). Mental health program evaluation: A multicomponent, multiperspective mixed method approach. In K. E. Robinson (Ed.), *Advances in school-based mental health interventions: Best practices and program models* (pp. 1–21). Kingston, NJ: Civic Research Institute.

National Center for Education Statistics. (2000). *Elementary and secondary education: An international perspective* (NCES 2000-033). Washington, DC: U.S. Department of Education.

National Research Council. (2005). *Advancing scientific research in education.* Washington, DC: National Academies Press.

Ogles, B. M., & Owens, J. S. (2004). Program evaluation: Developing outcome indicators for school-based mental health programs. In K. E. Robinson (Ed.), *Advances in school-based mental health interventions* (pp. 10–17). Kingston, NJ: Civic Research Institute.

Ostrom, C. W., Lerner, R. M., & Freel, M. A. (1995). Building the capacity of youth and families through university–community collaborations: The development-in-context evaluation (DICE) model. *Journal of Adolescent Research, 10,* 427–448.

Pelham, W. E., Massetti, G. M., & Waschbusch, D. A. (2007, June). *The academic and behavioral competencies program: Year 1 results of a school-wide comprehensive behavioral intervention.* Poster session presented at the annual meeting of the Institute of Education Sciences Research Conference, Washington, DC.

Petrosino, A. (2000). Mediators and moderators in the evaluation of programs for children: Current practice and agenda for improvement. *Evaluation Review, 24,* 47–72.

Porter, A. C., & Polikoff, M. S. (2007). NCLB: State interpretations, early effects, and suggestions for reauthorization. *Social Policy Report, 21,* 3–15.

Raudenbush, S. W. (1997). Statistical analysis and optimal design for group random-ized trials. *Psychological Methods, 2,* 173–185.

Raudenbush, S. W. (2003, November). *Designing field trials of educational innovations.* Paper presented at the national invitational conference, Conceptualizing Scale–UP: Multidisciplinary Perspectives, Washington, DC.

Raudenbush, S. W., Martinez, A., & Spybrook, J. (2007). Strategies for improving pre-cision in group-randomized experiments. *Educational Evaluation and Policy Analysis, 29,* 5–29.

Shadish, W. R., Cook, T. D., & Campbell, D. T. (2002). *Experimental and quasi-experimental designs for generalized causal inference.* Boston: Houghton Mifflin.

Snyder, T. D., Dillow, S. A., & Hoffman, C. M. (2007). *Digest of education statistics: 2006* (NCES 2007-017). Washington, DC: U.S. Government Printing Office.

St. Pierre, R. G., & Rossi, P. H. (2006). Randomize groups, not individuals: A strategy for improving early childhood programs. *Evaluation Review, 30,* 656–685.

Weiss, C. (1995). Nothing as practical as good theory: Exploring theory-based evaluation for comprehensive community initiatives for children and families. In J. P. Connell, A. C. Kubisch, L. B. Schorr, & C. H. Weiss (Eds.), *New approaches to evaluating community initiatives: Concepts, methods, and contexts* (pp. 65–92). Washington, DC: Aspen Institute.

White, P. A. (1990). Ideas about causation in philosophy and psychology. *Psychological Bulletin, 108,* 3–18.

U.S. Census Bureau. (2004). *Educational attainment in the United States: 2003.* Washington, DC: Author. Retrieved December 22, 2008, from http://www.census.gov/prod/2004pubs/p20-550.pdf

U.S. Department of Education. (2002). *No Child Left Behind.* Retrieved December 22, 2008, from http://www.ed.gov/nclb/landing.jhtml

U.S. Department of Education, Institute of Education Sciences. (2005). *What works clearinghouse.* Retrieved December 22, 2008, from http://ies.ed.gov/ncee/wwc/

U.S. Department of Education. (2006). *The condition of education: 2006* (NCES 2006-071). Washington, DC: U.S. Government Printing Office.

Yeaton, W. H., & Sechrest, L. (1981). Critical dimensions in the choice and maintenance of successful treatments: Strength, integrity, and effectiveness. *Journal of Consulting and Clinical Psychology, 49,* 156–167.

4

Conducting Classroom Observations in School-Based Research

Bridget K. Hamre, Robert C. Pianta,
and Lia Chomat-Mooney

There are few places in which children spend more time than classrooms, with the average child spending at least 15,000 hours in classrooms from the age of 4 or 5 until he or she leaves high school. Within classrooms, children and adolescents are exposed to critical experiences: They learn to read, write, and think critically; they make friends and have to face the inevitable challenges of peer relationships; and they are challenged to become productive, independent members of a larger society. Recently, there has been a significant increase in research activity devoted to examining the nature of students' experiences in classrooms and the ways in which these experiences contribute uniquely to social, cognitive, and academic development (see Pianta, 2006, for review).

Researchers from many disciplines are now spending time in classrooms. Developmental psychologists are interested in classrooms as one of the important settings in which development occurs. Prevention scientists, educational psychologists, and others are interested in classrooms as a location in which interventions and curricula are implemented and researched. Teacher educators and those who conduct research on alternative forms of teacher preparation are looking into classrooms to help detect whether their efforts to prepare teachers have been successful. With

This work was supported in part by a grant from the William T. Grant Foundation. The authors would like to thank Andrew Mashburn, Jason Downer, Amy Luckner, Kevin Grimm, and Tim Curby for their contributions to this work.

increased focus on accountability, even school administrators and policy researchers are looking to classrooms to yield information about the ingredients that will ensure student achievement.

Yet despite this broad interest in what happens inside classrooms, as well as a long history of this type of research (e.g., Brophy & Good, 1986), there is little consensus in the field about how to go about conducting classroom observations. Basic questions such as what should be measured and when to observe are most often left up to individual researchers, without a well-organized literature to help guide these decisions. In this chapter, we address some of these gaps in the literature and provide practical information for researchers on issues relevant to conducting classroom observations. Although researchers conduct classroom observations to obtain data on individual children and adolescents, the focus of this chapter is on the assessment of classroom-level variables such as instructional quality, implementation fidelity, and student–teacher relationships.

The chapter begins with a brief introduction to the history of classroom observation. We then provide a theory on classrooms that guide researchers deciding which aspects of classrooms are most important to observe. Next we discuss issues related to designing observational methodology. Then we explore the logistics of conducting classroom observations, addressing common areas of concern such as how long and when to observe to obtain a representative sample of the classroom environment. Consistent with the overall theme of the book, this section highlights ways in which observations can be conducted collaboratively with teachers and administrators. The last section discusses current limitations in classroom observation research and suggests several areas for future research and measure development.

HISTORY OF CLASSROOM OBSERVATION

Classroom observations have been used as measurement tools in educational research for more than 3 decades (Gage & Needels, 1989). The content and format of these observations have evolved in response to changing pressures exerted on researchers. Throughout the 1970s and

1980s, the majority of standardized classroom observations used in educational research studies were aligned with a paradigm referred to as *process-product research*. Seeking to better comprehend effective teaching, this research was composed primarily of correlational studies examining the relationships between classroom process variables, such as specific teacher behaviors, and student products or outcomes, namely student achievement. These studies were quantitative in nature and typically adopted observation schemes that used frequency counts of particular teacher behaviors to evaluate how the quantity of teaching related to the amount students learned (Brophy & Good, 1986).

Scholars within the educational research community criticized process–product research for its conceptual flaws as well as methodological and psychometric inadequacies (Gage, 1989). Conceptually, this research failed to adequately capture the complexity and depth of the classroom setting. One primary assumption of process–product research is that a linear, causal relationship exists between teacher behaviors and student outcomes. This underlying assumption placed emphasis on the specific, discrete behaviors of teachers and ignored the many other variables at play in the classroom environment (Gage, 1989). Correlational studies that attempted to isolate predictors of process–product relationships were often inconsistent or difficult to replicate (e.g., Gage & Needels, 1989). These problems further undermined the entire body of process-product research.

In reaction to these criticisms, researchers in the 1990s shied away from conducting quantitative studies using quantitative observation methods. Instead, qualitative observational methods were applied in research throughout the decade. These methods examined complex issues such as the degree to which classroom instruction was consistent with teachers' subject matter orientation and the ways in which teachers' and students' attitudes affected the implementation of curricula. This qualitative research provided rich, descriptive information about students' experiences in classrooms.

Most recently, the tide has shifted again in the direction of empirical educational research that incorporates standardized, quantitative observation systems. The Education Sciences Reform Act of 2002 established the Institute of Education Sciences (IES) within the U.S. Department of

Education with a mission to provide rigorous scientific evidence as a foundation for educational practice and policy decisions. As such, IES has
increased the availability of research funds in an effort to promote thorough quantitative studies whose findings will be generalizable to children
in schools. One critical area of inquiry continues to be the classroom environment. Private research entities, such as the William T. Grant Foundation and Spencer Foundation, have also pushed for a research agenda that
uses empirical techniques to examine the settings in which children live
and learn to better understand how these settings influence development.
In response to this call, scientists have placed renewed emphasis on developing classroom observational measures with adequate reliability and
validity (e.g., Cameron, Connor, & Morrison, 2005; Good, Mulryan, &
McCaslin, 2006; National Institute of Child Health and Human Development [NICHD] Early Child Care Research Network, 2002; Pianta, La
Paro, & Hamre, 2007; Pressley et al., 2003). Given this recent shift, and in
alignment with current funding priorities, most of the discussion that follows focuses on quantitative classroom observation measures; however,
much of the discussion is relevant to qualitative measurement as well.
Readers interested in more information on qualitative classroom observation measures are referred to Wragg (1999).

A THEORY OF CLASSROOM INTERACTIONS

An obvious first question for a researcher interested in classroom observations is what to observe. Some researchers are interested in classroom
observations because they are testing the effectiveness of a curricular package or intervention that is expected to change students' experiences in
classrooms. Others may be conducting more basic research on students'
development in classroom settings. Still others are interested in the classroom environment primarily as a potential moderator of interventions or
processes that occur outside the classroom. Although the content of observations is likely to vary depending on these different aims, a long history of
theory and research on social contexts and development (e.g., Bronfenbrenner & Morris, 1998; Eccles & Roeser, 1999; Pianta, 2006) provides
guidance to school-based researchers.

Focusing on Interactions

Classrooms are complex places. Researchers may be tempted to measure what is easy rather than what is most meaningful. As a result, some classroom observation tools focus more on materials available in the classrooms than on the complex nature of human interaction within these settings. Although there may be specific reasons for looking at the presence of materials in classrooms, research and developmental theory suggest that classroom observations will be most useful if they focus on the process and quality of students' actual experiences in the classroom. The underlying principle here is the idea of *proximal processes*. Bronfenbrenner and Morris (1998) advanced the notion that proximal processes— interactions that take place between children and their environment over time—serve as the primary mechanism for children's development. This theory, as applied to schooling, suggests that classroom interactions between adults and students and among students should be a primary focus of study when seeking to understand students' development in school contexts (Pianta, 2006). Examples of proximal processes in classrooms include teachers' interactions with students around behavior management, questioning and feedback during instruction, and the presence of supportive peer interactions. Thus, for example, if research is focusing on the literacy and language environment in the classroom, an observational tool that focuses solely on the presence of curricular materials is not likely to provide as much explanatory power (in terms of variations in implementation between teachers or in terms of effects on students) as a tool that assesses the ways to which these materials are used to transmit knowledge to students. The next section provides a developmentally based and empirically supported framework for delineating which types of interactions in classrooms are most proximal to students' development.

The framework presented below addresses some of the critiques of earlier process–product classroom observation work. Process–product research was informed by a behavioralist perspective and therefore relied on measures of discrete, behavioral indicators of putatively effective teaching (e.g., time allocations, presence of advanced organizers, number of instructional cues). The model proposed by Hamre and Pianta (2007), however, provides a developmental perspective and groups these more discrete behaviors into meaningful patterns of interaction predicated on proximal processes that developmental theory would suggest to be important for growth in academic and social outcomes (Pianta, 2006). This developmental approach to understanding classrooms is consistent with trends across the educational research agenda, such as the exemplary work of the National Research Council's series, *How Students Learn* (Donovan & Bransford, 2005), which summarizes research across disciplines to emphasize how specific teaching strategies can enhance students' development and application of these core thinking skills.

Three Major Domains of Classroom Interaction

To help organize the diverse literatures that inform what to observe within classroom environments, Hamre and Pianta (2007) proposed a system for organizing the wide range of interactions in classrooms, referred to as the Classroom Assessment Scoring System (CLASS) framework. The CLASS framework is a theoretically driven and empirically supported conceptualization of classroom interactions organized into three major domains: emotional supports, classroom organization, and instructional supports. Within each domain are a set of more specific dimensions of classroom interactions that are presumed to be important to students' academic and/or social development (see Table 4.1). The CLASS framework is consistent with several other descriptions of classroom environments put forth in the educational and developmental literatures (e.g., Brophy & Good, 1986; Eccles & Roeser, 1999; Pressley et al., 2003).

The CLASS framework is described briefly below as a way of synthesizing and organizing empirical evidence on the components of classrooms that are most proximal to students' experiences within those environments. Given the breadth of this model, we expect most researchers could locate their interests within this larger framework. Furthermore, the literature reviewed within each domain provides a good starting point for those interested in ways in which classrooms contribute to students' development. Table 4.1 provides practical information for researchers interested in knowing the specific types of classroom interactions that may be observed within each broad domain.

Table 4.1

Components of the Classroom Assessment Scoring System (CLASS) Framework for Classroom Quality

Domain	Dimension	Specific interactions and behaviors (teacher and student)
Emotional support	Positive climate	Positive affect, proximity, verbal and physical affection, cooperation, respectful language, eye contact
	Negative climate	Negative affect, irritability, aggression, threats, harsh punishment, teasing, bullying
	Teacher sensitivity	Anticipation of problem, provision of comfort and reassurance, effective resolution of difficulties, students taking risks, students seeking support
	Regard for student perspectives	Flexibility, incorporation of student ideas, provision of student choices, elicitation of student ideas, allowing movement
Classroom management	Behavior management	Clear expectations, consistency of enforcement, anticipation of behavior problems, attention to positive behaviors, efficient redirection of mild misbehavior, frequent compliance to rules
	Productivity	Few disruptions, efficient pacing, clear instructions, little student wandering, efficient transitions, materials ready and easily accessible
	Instructional learning formats	Teacher involvement, range of materials, active listening, use of advanced organizers, hands-on opportunities

(continued)

Table 4.1

Components of the Classroom Assessment Scoring System (CLASS) Framework for Classroom Quality (*Continued*)

Domain	Dimension	Specific interactions and behaviors (teacher and student)
Instructional support	Concept development	Use of why/how questions, problem solving, prediction, brainstorming, integration of concepts, real-world applications
	Quality of feedback	Hints, follow-up questions, students prompted for explanations, provision of clarification, recognition and reinforcement of effort
	Language modeling	Use of conversational strategies, open-ended questions, repetition and expansion of student comments, use of variety of language

Note. Data from Pianta, La Paro, & Hamre, 2007.

Emotional Support. Teacher efforts to support students' social and emotional functioning in the classroom, through positive facilitation of teacher–student and student–student interactions, are key elements of effective classroom practice. Two broad areas of developmental theory guide much of the work on emotional support in classrooms: attachment (e.g., Ainsworth, Blehar, Waters, & Wall, 1978) and self-determination theory (e.g., Ryan & Deci, 2000). Attachment theorists posit that when parents provide emotional support and a predictable, consistent, and safe environment, children become more self-reliant and are able to take risks as they explore the world because they know that an adult will be there to help them if they need it (Ainsworth et al., 1978). This theory has been broadly applied to and validated in school environments (see Pianta, Hamre, & Stuhlman, 2003, for review). Self-determination (or self-systems) theory

(Ryan & Deci, 2000) suggests that children are most motivated to learn when adults support their need to feel competent, positively related to others, and autonomous. Throughout schooling, students who are more motivated and connected to teachers and peers demonstrate positive trajectories of development in both social and academic domains (e.g., Ladd & Dinella, in press). As noted in Table 4.1, researchers interested in assessing classrooms' emotional climate may observe behaviors such as the teachers' and students' affect, verbal and nonverbal communications, and physical proximity, as well as the teachers' responsiveness to student concerns and provision of opportunities for students to take on leadership roles.

Classroom Organization. Educational research and practice place tremendous emphasis on the role of organization and management in creating a well-functioning classroom (e.g., Emmer & Strough, 2001). In the CLASS framework, classroom organization is a broad domain of classroom processes related to the organization and management of students' behavior, time, and attention in the classroom. From a developmental standpoint, research on children's self-regulatory skills provides the theoretical underpinnings of this domain (e.g., Raver, 2004), including focus on the development of memory, attention, planning, and inhibitory control, all of which have clear relevance to success in classroom environments. Classrooms that use more effective behavior management strategies, have more organized and routine management structures, and implement strategies that make students active participants in classroom activities have less oppositional behavior and higher levels of engagement in learning, and, ultimately, students who learn more. Researchers interested in assessing the quality of classroom organization and management may observe behaviors such as how frequently teachers make reactive comments to student behaviors, how often students are off task, how effectively the students transition from one activity to another, and how effectively a teacher uses instructional materials to engage students in learning (refer to Table 4.1 for more examples).

Instructional Support. Instructional methods have been put in the spotlight in recent years, as more emphasis has been placed on the translation of cognitive science, learning, and developmental research to educational environments. The theoretical foundation for the conceptualization of instructional supports in the CLASS framework comes primarily from research on children's cognitive and language development (e.g., Taylor, Pearson, Peterson, & Rodriguez, 2003). This literature highlights the distinction between simply learning facts and gaining "usable knowledge," which is built upon learning how facts are interconnected, organized, and conditioned on one another (Mayer, 2002). A student's cognitive and language development is contingent on the opportunities adults provide to express existing skills and scaffold more complex ones (e.g., Davis & Miyake, 2004). The development of "metacognitive" skills, or the awareness and understanding of one's thinking processes, is also critical to children's academic development. Examples of aspects of instruction that may be important to observe include the degree to which instruction is rote versus meaning-based, whether a teacher asks open (e.g., Why do you think the character ran away from home?) versus closed (e.g., What did the character take with him when he left home?) questions, how often students receive feedback about their work, and the degree to which the classroom is dominated by teacher-talk versus characterized by frequent conversations among students and teachers (refer to Table 4.1 for more examples). The instructional supports described earlier are general instructional strategies, relevant across content areas. However, there are also subsets of instructional supports that are specific to content areas such as reading, math, and science.

OBSERVATIONAL METHODOLOGY

Once researchers have decided what to observe, they must determine how to most effectively and efficiently measure classroom environments. At this point, researchers face a variety of decisions that have important implications for resulting data. Should measures assess the frequency or quality of behaviors? How should researchers make decisions about using existing measures versus designing their own? Finally, if designing an observational measure, what strategies should researchers use to ensure the measure meets the intended goals? We address each of these issues in the following sections, providing practical suggestions for researchers.

Frequency Versus Quality

Most observational measures of classroom environments focus either on the frequency or quality of observable processes or content. Examples of behaviors assessed by frequency (or time-sampled) measures include time spent on literacy instruction, the number of times teachers ask questions during instructional conversations, and the number of negative comments made by peers to one another. Quality measures may instead rate the degree to which literacy instruction in a classroom matches a description of evidence-based practices, how much instructional conversations stimulate children's higher order thinking skills, and the extent to which classroom interactions contain a high degree of negativity between teachers and students and among peers.

Frequency measures typically rely on time sampling methods, whereas quality is assessed using rating systems; however, this distinction can sometimes be blurred. Some measures that rely on assessing the presence of certain behaviors or interactions can focus on behaviors that have a quality component to them (e.g., Cameron et al., 2005). Similarly, many quality measures take into account the frequency of a group of behaviors in making the quality rating (NICHD Early Child Care Research Network, 2002; Pianta et al., 2007).

There are advantages and disadvantages to each type of system. Quality measures assess higher order organizations of behaviors in ways that may be more meaningful than looking at the discrete behaviors in isolation and tend to parse the behavioral stream into more contextually and situationally sensitive "chunks." For example, teachers' positive affect and smiling can have different meanings and may be interpreted differently depending on the ways in which this affect is responded to by students in the classroom. In some classrooms teachers are exceptionally cheerful, but their affect appears very disconnected from that of the students. In other classrooms teachers are more subdued in their positive affect, but there is a clear match between this affect and those of their students. A measure that simply counted the number of times a teacher smiled at students would miss these more nuanced interpretations. One distinct advantage to using frequency measures, specifically when they are time-coded, is the ability to conduct sequential and contingency analyses, thus allowing for studies of the complex interdependence and flow of interactions (Bakeman & Gnisci, 2006), though these analyses are not common in educational literatures.

One other difference between these two approaches concerns the degree to which they are subject to observer effects. A recent report compared the two methods of classroom observation and determined that of the two observational strategies, there tend to be more significant observer effects using global ratings of classroom interactions than time samplings of more discrete behaviors (Chomat-Mooney et al., 2008). This report examined global ratings and time-sampled behaviors (of teachers and students) observed in more than 3,000 classrooms (pre-K–Grade 5) that were a part of the NICHD Study of Early Child Care and Youth Development (see http://secc.rti.org/ for much more detailed information on this study). Within classrooms in this study, approximately 4% to 14% of the variance in classroom quality ratings was attributed to observers compared with approximately 1% to 7% of the variance in frequency codes. This finding is not surprising given that quality ratings tend to require greater levels of inference than do frequency approaches. Counting the number of times a teacher smiles requires much less inference than does making a holistic judgment about the degree to which a teacher fostered a positive classroom climate. This point emphasizes the need for adequate training and strategies for maintaining reliability among classroom observers, issues considered in greater detail in the next few sections.

Another factor to consider, however, is how much of the variance in these ratings can be attributed to stable characteristics of the classroom versus factors that change over time as a result of things such as subject matter, number of students, and time of day. Chomat-Mooney et al. (2008) presented results suggesting that time-sampled codes in the NICHD Study of Early Child Care and Youth Development showed little classroom-level variance, indicating that these codes were not as sensitive to differences between teachers and classrooms as were the global ratings. More specifically, most of the variance in time-sampled codes was found at the cycle level, suggesting that a large amount of variance in time-sampled codes came from differences from one cycle to the next for the same teacher. The high degree of cycle-level variance found in time-sampled codes suggests that this approach to coding is sensitive to fluctuations in classroom activities or time of day rather than stable aspects of the teachers' behavior. The global ratings, on the other hand, showed less cycle-to-cycle variance and more teacher-level variability, indicating these codes better capture aspects of teachers' behavior with students that can be attributed to them as individuals, or the classroom as a whole, rather than the situation. Researchers need to weigh each of these advantages and disadvantages in deciding on the most appropriate observational tool for their project.

Using Existing Measures Versus Designing New Measures

When embarking on a new project, researchers often face the challenge of deciding whether to use existing measures versus developing their own measures (refer to chap. 5, this volume, for a more complete discussion of this issue). In the vast majority of research including classroom observations to date, researchers have chosen the latter path. Consistent with the recommendations in chapter 5, we suggest making use of existing measures whenever possible. However, a stringent evaluation of these measures is critical. Researchers should consider four major factors as they evaluate existing tools. First, and most obviously, does the tool measure the constructs of interest? As noted earlier, there is a clear tradeoff here because rarely will an existing measure exactly map onto researchers' constructs of interest. However, researchers might consider a compromise by using an existing measurement system and supplementing it with a few additional scales or frequency codes that are more specific to the project.

A second factor that researchers should consider in evaluating observational tools concerns evidence of the tool's *reliability*. Reliability is an essential characteristic of a good observation tool, because if the tool does not measure things consistently, or reliably, then one cannot assume that the scores are an accurate reflection of the actual classroom processes. Unlike for some other measures, such as questionnaires, it is not sufficient to simply find tools that have shown adequate reliability in other studies. The use of observational methodology requires establishing acceptable levels of reliability within each project. This typically requires some degree of training for observational data collectors. Thus, one way to assess the feasibility of using an existing observational system is to consider whether the tool provides a standardized process for training observers to make reliable judgments about what they attend to and record in the classroom. Given the complexity of classrooms, most training procedures for classroom observation tools take substantial time, ranging from a few days to several weeks or even months. Obviously, the length of time it takes to establish reliability for observers is one factor to consider in deciding whether to use a given tool.

A third factor to consider is whether measure developers provide a test for potential observers to certify that they meet a preset reliability criterion. How should researchers go about setting this reliability criterion? Here researchers must weigh the tradeoffs between feasibility and reliability. It is clear that obtaining the highest degree of reliability possible is the target, and measure developers often establish a criterion, but researchers must make their own decisions about this for their projects. In our experience it is worth investing some extra time and resources into establishing and maintaining high levels of reliability. Although the investment of time and money can be substantial, going forward with observations without clear evidence of reliability will undermine the usefulness of observation data.

A final consideration in choosing an observational tool concerns validity. There are many types of validity, but two seem most critical in the case of classroom observation. *Content* validity assesses the degree to which the measure captures the construct of interest. For example, if a researcher is interested in assessing the quality of peer interactions in the classroom, he or she would need to assess the degree to which existing classroom observational measures paid attention to the specific types of peer interactions of interest. A second major component of validity to attend to is *predictive* validity—in this case, is the observational measure associated with student outcomes of interest? In the example above, a researcher who is interested in the extent to which peer interactions in the classroom may contribute to the development of children's internalizing symptoms will want to investigate the extent to which the potential measures of peer interactions have been associated with internalizing symptoms in previous research.

How to Design a New Observational Measure:
The Case of Measuring Implementation

If a researcher decides to design a new observational measure, he or she should consider several factors. Our experience suggests that one of the most common reasons researchers decide to design their own measure is that they are interested in assessing the effectiveness of a curricula or intervention and are in need of an implementation measure that is specific to the particular curricula or intervention. Therefore, in this section we use the case of designing an observational measure of implementation as an example of some of the issues that arise in this process; however, the issues are relevant regardless of the type of measure being designed.

The first step in designing an observational tool is to establish the constructs of interest. This typically requires a relatively extensive review of relevant literature. For example, in the development of the CLASS framework, we used the theoretical model presented earlier to help organize an exhaustive review of empirical studies that linked specific classroom behaviors to student outcomes. In the case of implementation, a review of the relevant literature would lead researchers to one of the constructs most relevant to an observational tool, which is often referred to as *quality of delivery* (Greenberg, Domitrovich, Graczyk, & Zins, 2005). Quality of delivery describes the nature of teachers' engagement with the intervention, the use of effective teaching strategies, and teachers' ability to generalize the intervention to interactions throughout the school day. Unfortunately, as noted by Greenberg and colleagues, there is not yet consensus on how best to go about measuring quality of delivery.

One of the most challenging parts of designing an observational measure is to delineate the specific behavioral markers of interest. As stated by Gersten, Baker, and Lloyd (2000), "Researchers often have a very good conceptual sense of what they would like to see during instruction, but only 'half formed images' of the types of specific actions and behaviors that constitute the implementation on a day-by-day, minute-to-minute basis" (p. 9). There is no magic answer as to how to move from these half-formed images to behaviors that could be reliably assessed in classrooms, and our experience suggests that this is a long and iterative process. A good starting point is to videotape a broad range of teachers implementing the curriculum or intervention, with a focus on finding teachers who are known to be effective and ineffective implementers. Careful review of these videos by intervention developers and people with classroom teaching experience may yield consensus around a set of specific practices indicative of high- and low-quality implementation. These behaviors can then be included in an observational protocol that is tested systematically to assess reliability and validity. In an initial pilot of the measure, it is likely that there will be some behaviors that, although deemed important, are too hard for people to reliably judge or happen too infrequently to adequately sample during classroom observations. Several revisions of the measure are likely before adequate reliability and validity are obtained.

LOGISTICAL ISSUES IN CLASSROOM OBSERVATIONS

Once researchers have determined what to observe and decided on the observational tool or tools they will use, there are myriad logistical issues to consider. This discussion of logistical issues comes from our own extensive experience with classroom observation. Unfortunately, few published studies offer guidance to researchers about these kinds of practical issues. However, they are the types of issues that we, as the developers of an observational tool, are asked again and again. As a result, we have recently begun to examine some of these practical issues with data from our observational studies in over 4,000 early childhood and elementary classrooms (Chomat-Mooney et al., 2008). In some cases we have included data from other projects (e.g., Cappella, Watling, & Atkins, 2008; Jones, Brown, & Aber, 2008; Rimm-Kaufman & Chiu, 2007); however, all of these projects use similar observational protocols, relying either on the Classroom Observation System (COS) developed for the NICHD Study of Early Child Care and Youth Development (NICHD Early Child Care Research Network, 2002) or the CLASS framework developed by Pianta et al. (2007). Although these studies provide the most comprehensive classroom observation data available today, they are limited by the use of only two measures of observation and, more notably, by the fact that we have limited data on middle school and secondary classrooms. Although we expect many of the issues discussed below would generalize to other measures of classrooms, this has yet to be examined empirically.

The CLASS and COS both have established training protocols, as well as reliability and validity (e.g., Hamre & Pianta, 2005; Mashburn et al., in press). Each measure includes ratings of major dimensions of classroom interactions (on a 1–7 scale); the COS also includes time-sampled teacher and student behaviors. Readers are referred to technical documents for the CLASS (Pianta et al., 2007) and COS (NICHD Early Child Care Research Network, 2002) for more information.

Stability of Classrooms Across Days

A primary question concerns the number of observations that need to be completed to adequately sample classroom-level processes. This issue is critical because classroom observations are expensive and time consuming for researchers and often inconvenient for schools and teachers. The number of observations needed is obviously dependent on a variety of factors, including the measures used and research questions. However, research from several large studies of classrooms suggests that, at least at the preschool and elementary level, classroom processes are fairly stable over time. For example, within a study of 240 preschool classrooms (Pianta et al., 2007), observers returned to classroom for 2 days in a row. Stability of Day 1 and Day 2 ratings on the CLASS dimensions estimated with zero-order correlations ranged from .73 to .85.

Stability of Classrooms Within a Day

The studies cited above typically observed in classrooms for an entire school day; however, this often exceeds the capacity of research budgets, and there is an interest in assessing the amount of time needed within a particular day to get a reliable estimate of the classroom environment. As reported by Chomat-Mooney et al. (2008) and Pianta et al. (2007), analyses of several data sets suggest that four to six cycles of observation (each cycle being 15–20 minutes observation time and 5–10 minutes of coding time) typically produce estimates of classroom processes that are highly correlated ($r = .82-.93$) with scores obtained during an entire school day.

There do appear to be minor fluctuations in classroom processes across the school day, and thus it is important to try to measure a consistent time of day across the sample of classrooms. In particular, the beginning of the day, at least in elementary classrooms, tends to look fairly different compared with later time points. Most teachers start the day by dealing with managerial routines (e.g., taking attendance, collecting lunch money) and so, not surprising, instructional activities are far less likely to occur at the very beginning of the school day, and global ratings related to instruction in the classroom are lower (Chomat-Mooney et al., 2008). However, this may be an important time to observe in classrooms because the way in which teachers manage this time can be an important indicator of their teaching skills. To ensure that variation in the time of day the observational data are collected does not affect scores, a systematic decision should be made with regard to including or not including this first part of the day.

Stability of Classrooms Across the Year

A related issue concerns the timing of classroom observations across the school year. In general, there appears to be moderate stability in observations from the fall to spring of the school year (Chomat-Mooney et al., 2008; Pianta et al., 2007); however, there do appear to be times in which classroom practices are less likely to look like they do the rest of the year. Classrooms appear have more management activities, and less instruction, at the beginning of the year (Hamre, Pianta, Mashburn, & Downer, 2007), and the quality of classroom organization and management drops in the last few months of school, at least within a sample of preschool classrooms observed repeatedly over a year (Hamre et al., 2007). These systematic changes over the course of a year emphasize the need for intervention studies to include observations of both control and treatment classrooms to avoid attributing natural fluctuations in classroom process to intervention effects.

Method of Classroom Observation: Live Versus Videotape

Another set of issues concerns the method of data collection. The majority of classroom research conducted to date has relied on live observations. However, recent advancements in digital technology make it more feasible to use videotaped observations. One application of this method of classroom observation, the MyTeachingPartner project, provided video cameras to hundreds of preschool (Pianta et al., in press) and middle and high school (Allen & Pianta, 2008) teachers. Teachers were asked to videotape their classrooms and mail the videotapes to researchers every other week across a 2-year period. This strategy minimizes the cost of observation (e.g., travel time for observers) and saves time related to coordinating observations. Initial evidence suggests that ratings made from these videotape observations are consistent with those using live observation procedures (Pianta et al., 2007). Use of videotape also has the advantage of providing researchers with greater flexibility in coding. For example, it is possible to cycle through the video multiple times, watch the behavior of a different child on each cycle, and thus build a database in which there are linked behavioral sequences for the teacher and multiple children in the classroom. The availability of videotape also allows for researchers to pilot several different observation strategies with their sample prior to making a final decision. There are limitations to using video captured by teachers. Because of sound and camera placement issues, it is challenging for teachers to adequately capture group work. In addition, teachers who film themselves have opportunities to edit what they send or retape if they are unhappy with the way a particular lesson was implemented. Therefore, if funds are available, it may be better to send a data collector into the classroom to collect video.

Assigning Observers to Classrooms

One of the most common questions we receive from those conducting classroom observations concerns how to assign observers to classrooms. Unless a tool provides perfect reliability or 100% agreement across observers, there will be some observer effects. One way to help reduce the effects of observers on data is to randomly assign observers to classrooms. For example, imagine a case in which researchers are interested in assessing the degree to which schools within four districts within a state offer different levels of classroom quality. Often, to reduce travel times, project planners will assign a set of coders to each district. Even though all coders have been trained, passed reliability tests, and participated in drift test sessions (see next section for more discussion on drift), coders assigned to District A may tend to score slightly higher than those assigned to Districts B, C, and D. Researches may then mistakenly conclude that District A has classrooms of higher quality. Random assignment of coders to districts would avoid this potential problem. Another way to reduce the effect of observers on classroom observational data is to consider assigning multiple observers per classroom.

The issue of random assignment is particularly important within intervention studies. Of course, observers should be blind to conditions in randomized trials. In addition, observers should be randomly assigned to conditions, so that every observer is in some treatment and some control classrooms. One advantage to using videotape for classroom intervention research is that it allows projects to delay coding until all the data are in (e.g., pre- and posttreatment observations) in ways that allow for more systematic randomization of coders across conditions and time. This is particularly important because almost all projects have observer turnovers. If, for example, one set of observers codes preintervention classrooms and another set of observers codes postintervention classrooms, systematic observer effects may be misinterpreted as significant intervention effects or may conceal real effects of the intervention.

Maintaining and Assessing Reliability Among Observers

As discussed previously, most classroom observational tools require intensive initial training to ensure that potential observers meet an established reliability criterion. However, researchers are often interested in collecting classroom observations over several months or years. These longer data collection periods bring up concerns related to *drift* among observers, or the tendency for observers to move away from being reliable observers using a particular tool. Drift occurs as observers make ratings day after day and begin to internalize their own definitions for specific codes or scales in ways that may or may not be consistent with the measure's definitions. There are several ways to help prevent substantial drift. In general, we recommend researchers institute drift procedures for data collection occurring for more than 2 months. The most effective way to address drift is to have all observers convene on a regular basis during data collection to code together and discuss these codes. Ideally, projects have access to video segments coded by measure developers for this purpose to prevent entire sets of observers from drifting together away from the metrics set by the measure. However, in the absence of this type of video, projects may use any available video. Observers should code this video in the same way they would for data collection and then engage in a discussion of areas where there was disagreement. This process can be conducted in person, or videos can be made available to observers in the field and discussion can occur through conference calls. Individual observers then need to receive feedback on whether their scoring remains consistent with others in the project.

Projects should also plan for a certain percentage of observations to be double coded. This will involve either sending two observers into a classroom simultaneously or, if using video, assigning a portion of tapes to be double coded. Although there are no data to suggest an ideal percentage, we generally recommend that between 15% and 20% of all observations are double coded.

Collaborating With Schools and Teachers

A final set of logistical issues concern the ways in which researchers can effectively collaborate with schools and teachers to conduct classroom observations. The discussion of the issues below stems from years of collaborative work with teachers in this area.

Minimizing Disruptions

Researchers need to make every effort to minimize the disruption that observations can cause to teachers and students. A veteran teacher, who has participated in numerous research projects, makes the following recommendations for classroom observers:

1. If possible, arrange to start the observation at the beginning of the day or during a transition so that work time is not disrupted. Make sure to be on time.
2. Talk with the teacher ahead of time about how he or she should introduce the observer.
3. Answer students' questions directly but succinctly. A simple statement such as "I'm just here to take notes on what is happening in your classroom" usually suffices. Avoid comments suggesting you are evaluating the behavior of students or teachers. If a student persists in asking questions, refer them to their teacher.
4. If using a video camera, try to minimize the amount the camera moves around, as this tends to distract students from their activities. Watch any cords so that the camera does not become a safety hazard.

Sharing Information With Teachers

Researchers often wonder how much information about what they are observing should be shared with teachers. This may range from simple descriptions of the types of things that observers are coding to detailed records of the actual results from observations of an individual classroom. Here researchers must balance a desire to build a collaborative relationship with schools with the potential consequences of sharing such information. In intervention work, researchers are often concerned about the effect that sharing information may have on teachers' practice; providing teachers with a detailed rubric of aspects of high-quality implementation of an intervention, for example, may lead teachers to try to emulate these behaviors in ways they would not have otherwise. In more basic research this may be less of a concern. However, even in the context of basic research, it is often more confusing than helpful to provide teachers with a detailed reporting of results from an observation, particularly because data collectors are generally not qualified to provide meaningful feedback to teachers about what these observations may mean. In general, researchers should try to share as much information as possible without biasing the sample. Often this is accomplished by sharing aggregate results of the study to participants after the data collection is complete.

Developing a Plan for Troubling Situations

Almost everyone who has engaged in classroom observation has had to deal with the issue of what to do when a data collector observes something troubling during the course of observations. This may include observations such as a teacher threatening or hitting a student, a student victimizing a peer, or a dangerous environmental hazard. By developing a plan for how to deal with these types of observations prior to data collection, researchers can avoid potentially uncomfortable situations with teachers and schools. It is helpful to sit down with school personnel (a research coordinator or administrator) and develop a plan for reporting these incidents. Topics to discuss include which types of incidents require reporting, how that reporting should be completed, and to whom. Ultimately, decisions on whether to disclose such incidents depend on a number of factors and must be made on a case-by-case basis; however, articulating a plan ahead of time will help build a sense of collaboration between researchers and schools. University institutional review boards can be a helpful source for consultation when these issues arise.

LIMITATIONS AND FUTURE DIRECTIONS

Despite the interest in classrooms and the recent resurgence in classroom observation methodologies, many unanswered questions remain. In particular, there is a greater need to understand how to most effectively measure middle and high school classrooms. These classrooms are organized differently from elementary classrooms, and conducting observations in these settings brings up new challenges, such as the fact that most middle school and secondary teachers teach multiple cohorts of students. Should interventions that target secondary teachers focus on observing the teacher during one specific class period or on observing the teacher in multiple contexts? How big of an effect does classroom composition have on the quality of the classroom environment?

Another concern relates to issues of reliability and validity. Although measures such as COS and CLASS have been shown to relate to student outcomes, the effect sizes tend to be modest (Hamre & Pianta, 2005; Mashburn et al., in press). This is likely due to a variety of factors, but measurement issues are paramount. Finding ways to reduce error in measurements of classroom observation (e.g., observer effects) would enhance the precision of these estimates. Furthermore, there is a need for greater precision related to the constructs within classrooms that have greatest salience for specific student outcomes. Measures can then be developed to reliably and validly assess these constructs. To be most useful, these measures need to have the capacity to be scaled for use in large research projects (e.g., reasonable training times, manualized training).

Finally, classroom observations continue to be an expensive research endeavor. This fact prevents many school-based researchers from including classroom observations. It will be important for future work to find ways to reduce the cost of classroom observation, perhaps through innovative technology such as streaming video and the use of automated video-coding software.

Despite these limitations, there is now clear evidence demonstrating how critical it is to include observational assessments in school-based research. Classroom observations have been a primary method through which we can understand, measure, model, and aim to improve the social, instructional, and motivational processes that are responsible for supporting the value that schooling has for all involved.

REFERENCES

Ainsworth, M. D., Blehar, M. C., Waters, E., & Wall, D. (1978). *Patterns of attachment: A psychological study of the Strange Situation.* Hillsdale, NJ: Erlbaum.

Allen, J., & Pianta, R. C. (2008). Building capacity for positive youth development in secondary school classrooms: Changing teachers' interactions with students. In M. Shinn & H. Yoshikawa (Eds.), *Changing schools and community organizations to foster positive youth development* (pp. 21–39). New York: Oxford University Press.

Bakeman, R., & Gnisci, A. (2006). Sequential observation methods. In M. Eid & E. Diener (Eds.), *Handbook of multimethod measurement in psychology* (pp. 127–140). Washington, DC: American Psychological Association.

Bronfenbrenner, U., & Morris, P. A. (1998). The ecology of developmental processes. In W. Damon & R. M. Lerner (Eds.), *Handbook of child psychology: Vol. 1. Theoretical models of human development* (5th ed., pp. 993–1029). New York: Wiley.

Brophy, J. E., & Good, T. L. (1986). Teacher behavior and student achievement. In M. C. Wittrock (Ed.), *Handbook of research on teaching* (3rd ed., pp. 328–375). New York: Macmillan.

Cameron, C. E., Connor, C. M., & Morrison, F. J. (2005). Effects of variation in teacher organization on classroom functioning. *Journal of School Psychology, 43*, 61–85.

Cappella, E., Watling N. J., & Atkins, M. S. (2008, March). *Links to learning: Teacher practices and student social networks in urban classrooms.* Paper presented at the annual meeting of the American Educational Research Association, New York, NY.

Chomat-Mooney, L. I., Pianta, R. C., Hamre, B. K., Mashburn, A. J., Luckner, A. E., Grimm, K. J., et al. (2008). *A practical guide for conducting classroom observations: A summary of issues and evidence for school-based researchers.* New York: William T. Grant Foundation.

Davis, E. A., & Miyake, N. (2004). Explorations of scaffolding in complex classroom systems. *Journal of the Learning Sciences, 13*, 265–272.

Donovan, S., & Bransford, J. (2005). *How students learn.* Washington, DC: National Academies Press, National Research Council.

Eccles, J. S., & Roeser, R. W. (1999). Adolescents' perceptions of middle school: Relation to longitudinal changes in academic and psychological adjustment. *Journal of Research on Adolescence, 8*, 123–158.

Emmer, E. T., & Strough, L. (2001). Classroom management: A critical part of educational psychology, with implications for teacher education. *Educational Psychologist, 36*, 103–112.

Gage, N. L. (1989). The paradigm wars and their aftermath: A "historical" sketch of research on teaching since 1989. *Educational Researcher, 18*(7), 4–10.

Gage, N. L., & Needels, M. C. (1989). Process–product research on teaching: A review of criticisms. *Elementary School Journal, 89*, 253–300.

Gersten, R., Baker, S., & Lloyd, J. W. (2000). Designing high quality research in special education: Group experimental design. *Journal of Special Education, 34*, 2–18.

Good, T., Mulryan, C., & McCaslin, M. (2006). Grouping for instruction in mathematics: A call for programmatic research on small-group processes. In D. Grouws (Ed.), *Handbook of research on mathematics teaching and learning* (pp. 165–196). New York: Macmillan.

Greenberg, M. T., Domitrovich, C. E., Graczyk, P. A., & Zins, J. E. (2005). *Promotion of mental health and prevention of mental and behavioral disorders: Vol. 3. The study of implementation in school-based preventive interventions: Theory, research, and practice.* Rockville, MD: Center for Mental Health Services, Substance Abuse and Mental Health Services Administration.

Hamre, B. K., & Pianta, R. C. (2005). Can instructional and emotional support in the first grade classroom make a difference for children at risk of school failure? *Child Development, 76,* 949–967.

Hamre, B. K., & Pianta, R. C. (2007). Learning opportunities in preschool and early elementary classrooms. In R. C. Pianta, M. J. Cox, & K. Snow (Eds.), *School readiness and the transition to school* (pp. 49–84). Baltimore: Paul H. Brookes.

Hamre, B. K., Pianta, R., Mashburn, A., & Downer, J. (2007, March). *Growth models of classroom quality over the course of the year in preschool programs.* Paper presented at the biennial meeting of the Society for Research in Child Development, Boston, MA.

Jones, S. M., Brown, J. L., & Aber, J. L. (2008). Classroom settings as targets of intervention and research. In M. Shinn & Yoshikawa, H. (Eds.), *Changing schools and community organizations to foster positive youth development* (pp. 58–77). New York: Oxford University Press.

Ladd, G. W., & Dinella, L. (in press). Continuity and change in early school engagement: Predictive of children's achievement trajectories from first to eighth grade? *Journal of Educational Psychology.*

Mashburn, A. J., Pianta, R. C., Hamre, B. K., Downer, J. T., Barbarin, O., Bryant, D., et al. (in press). Measures of classroom quality in pre-kindergarten and children's development of academic, language and social skills. *Child Development.*

Mayer, R. E. (2002). Rote versus meaningful learning. *Theory Into Practice, 41,* 226–233.

National Institute of Child Health and Human Development, Early Child Care Research Network. (2002). The relation of global first-grade classroom environment to structural classroom features and teacher and student behaviors. *Elementary School Journal, 102,* 367–387.

Pianta, R. C. (2006). Schools, schooling, and developmental psychopathology. In D. Cicchetti & D. Cohen (Eds.), *Developmental psychopathology: Vol. 1. Theory and method* (pp. 494–529). Hoboken, NJ: Wiley.

Pianta, R. C., Hamre, B., & Stuhlman, M. (2003). Relationships between teachers and children. In W. Reynolds & G. Miller (Eds.), *Comprehensive handbook of psychology: Vol. 7. Educational psychology* (pp. 199–234). Hoboken, NJ: Wiley.

Pianta, R. C., La Paro, K., & Hamre, B. K. (2007). *Classroom assessment scoring system.* Baltimore: Paul H. Brookes.

Pianta, R. C., Mashburn, A. J., Downer, J. T., Hamre, B. K., & Justice, L. (in press). Effects of web-mediated professional development resources on teacher–child interactions in pre-kindergarten classrooms. *Early Childhood Research Quarterly.*

Pressley, M., Roehrig, A., Raphael, L., Dolezal, S., Bohn, K., Mohan, L., et al. (2003). Teaching processes in elementary and secondary education. In W. M. Reynolds & G. E. Miller (Eds.), *Comprehensive handbook of psychology: Vol. 7. Educational psychology* (pp. 153–175). New York: Wiley.

Raver, C. C. (2004). Placing emotional self-regulation in sociocultural and socio-economic contexts. *Child Development, 75,* 346–353.

Rimm-Kaufman, S. E., & Chiu, Y. I. (2007). Promoting social and academic competence in the classroom: An intervention study examining the contribution of the responsive classroom approach. *Psychology in the Schools, 44,* 397–413.

Ryan, R. M., & Deci, E. L. (2000). Self-determination theory and the facilitation of intrinsic motivation, social development, and well-being. *American Psychologist, 55,* 68–78.

Taylor, B. M., Pearson, P. D., Peterson, D. S., & Rodriguez, M. C. (2003). Reading growth in high-poverty classrooms: The influence of teacher practices that encourage cognitive engagement in literacy learning. *Elementary School Journal, 104,* 3–28.

Wragg, E. C. (1999). *An introduction to classroom observation.* London: Routledge.

5

Choosing Measures for School-Based Research: Scientific and Practical Considerations

Amy Silverman, Jennifer Coyne Cassata,
Gary Gottfredson, and Sylvia Rosenfield

Deciding on the measures to be used in school-based research is a complex process that entails weighing numerous scientific and practical considerations that are frequently in conflict with each other. These conflicts arise as researchers and school personnel struggle to balance often competing priorities. This chapter offers practical guidelines and tips for how to navigate the process of choosing and developing measures and for mounting successful data collection effort in schools. It highlights the scientific and practical considerations that researchers and school representatives should think about before deciding whether to use existing measures, whether to adapt measures that currently exist in the scientific literature or school community, or whether to develop new measures. The idea is for researcher–school collaborations to be proactive during the planning phases of the research project rather than reactive when problems arise during data collection. Once measurement decisions are made, it is the researcher's responsibility to work collaboratively with school staff as problems arise so that measures can be adjusted as needed to optimize the benefits of the original measurement choices.

The chapter also describes some of the types and varieties of measures currently available to researchers conducting research in schools (including paper-and-pencil self-administered questionnaires, Web surveys, interviews, and archival data) and highlights the pros and cons of each type of measurement (see chap. 4, this volume, for information about observational techniques). In the second part of the chapter, we illustrate many of these measurement and data collection issues through a case example involving a large randomized control intervention trial occurring in 45 elementary schools within a Virginia school district (Rosenfield, Silva, & Gravois, 2008). The case example illustrates in a practical manner the communication and technical challenges that arose after a measurement decision was made to use Web survey technology and describes the collaborative, data-driven approach that researchers and the school district used to make measurement adjustments. The chapter also highlights our use of Web survey technology utilizing *Tailored Design Method* procedures (Dillman, 2000) that were adapted for this study. Written collaboratively by researchers and school personnel, the chapter offers both researcher and school-district perspectives on the strengths and weaknesses of this cutting-edge approach to measurement. Finally, we conclude with a discussion of the problems and barrier encountered, the lessons learned, and modifications that were made in the 2nd year of the project.

SCIENTIFIC AND RESEARCH CONSIDERATIONS

Researchers' choices in measures are driven by the goals of the study's research, the money and research staff time available to devote to measurement development, and the availability of information about the measures' psychometric properties (e.g., reliability and validity information). Additionally, researchers should undertake a comprehensive review of the scientific literature to determine whether currently existing measures adequately capture the constructs of interest for a particular study. Before moving too far along in this process, researchers need to allow adequate consulting time with school personnel to determine whether related measures already exist within the school community and to receive feedback as to whether proposed measures adequately capture the constructs of interest.

A benefit to using existing measures is that they can be selected based on adequate levels of reliability and validity and can save the researcher a substantial amount of time and money. A drawback to developing new measures is that this process can be time consuming and labor intensive, and it requires a level of psychometric/methodological sophistication that many researchers do not possess. For this reason, we recommend that researchers try to keep original measures with sound psychometric properties intact and add supplemental questions or scales that tap their specific project's construct or constructs of interest. At times, slight modifications to existing measures, such as the deletion of irrelevant items and/or making minor wording changes to make items more age appropriate, may be warranted. When using a new or adapted measure, researchers should consider using more than one measure so that the convergent validity of the new measure can be tested. This can also help ensure that information on a topic is not completely lost should one of the new measures be deemed flawed.

Regardless of whether researchers decide to develop new measures or use existing ones, some degree of piloting or pretesting of the questions is essential before going out in the field. Although pretesting has always been a highly touted part of questionnaire design, in practice it is often done haphazardly, if at all (Dillman, 2000). Some of the more common piloting or pretesting techniques used by researchers include (a) having knowledgeable colleagues review measures to examine the substantive content and wording of the questionnaire (e.g., reduce redundancy); (b) testing the measures on potential participants using think-out-loud techniques (e.g., asking participants to read the questions out loud and to tell the interviewer everything they are thinking) or retrospective interviewing techniques (e.g., asking respondents to complete the questionnaire as if the interviewer were not there and then interviewing them about potential problems); and (c) conducting a small pilot study to examine initial reliability and validity of the survey items, which will assist with finalizing response categories, reduce highly correlated items, and eliminate problematic skip patterns (Dillman, 2000). The size of this pilot study depends on project resources.

Choosing appropriate measures for use in schools also requires researchers to carefully consider the participants who will be receiving the measures. Response rates will be highest when measures use simple, understandable language that avoids double negatives and awkwardly worded items, and when the time required to complete the survey is kept to a minimum to avoid participant burnout and fatigue. Lengthy, redundant surveys have a tendency to frustrate school personnel and students and will likely result in poor data quality. A useful tool for researchers evaluating existing measures to determine whether to use them as is, adapt them, or develop new measures is Don Dillman's book, *Mail and Internet Surveys: The Tailored Design Method* (2000), which highlights principles for writing good survey questions. The *Tests in Print* and *Mental Measurements Yearbook* series are other helpful resources for identifying existing tests and inventories for use in school-based research.

Researchers using existing measures must determine whether the measures are in the public domain or whether the measures require permission from authors. Copyright laws frequently prohibit the use of measures without payment to authors or the publisher, and an e-mail exchange between the author and the researcher can assist with obtaining permission.

PRACTICAL/SCHOOL CONSIDERATIONS

From a school's perspective, practical considerations such as the time it takes staff to complete surveys or interviews, the timing of survey administration (e.g., beginning of school year, end of school year), confidentiality/anonymity issues (e.g., what steps will be taken to safeguard confidentiality of the respondents), and data ownership (e.g., who owns the data and what type of data/information will be shared or disseminated) are of paramount importance and should be discussed and decided on collaboratively well before data collection begins. School administrators, teachers, and staff are often concerned by the amount of time needed to administer a survey and whether a survey will interfere with teachers' instructional time. It is up to the researcher to provide a convincing rationale for how the school will benefit from participation in the research project early in the life of the project, well before data collection begins. See chapters 1 and 2 of this volume for more information.

TYPES OF MEASURES USED IN SCHOOL-BASED RESEARCH

A variety of measures are available to researchers conducting research in schools, each type offering its own set of advantages and disadvantages. Although the choice of measures ultimately depends on the research questions, budgetary constraints, and available resources, it is best for researchers to use a variety of measures instead of relying on one type of measure to understand the phenomenon of interest. We recommend including at least two types of measures to avoid the weaknesses inherent in a mono-method approach (Shadish, Cook, & Campbell, 2002) and to examine whether the evidence converges or diverges. In the following sections, we describe recent technological advances that may inform researchers' decisions about the most appropriate measurement strategies.

Paper-and-Pencil Self-Administered Questionnaires

The majority of research being conducted in schools over the past few decades has involved the use of traditional paper-and-pencil questionnaire or surveys administered to students, teachers, principals, and other school staff. Typically, researchers design surveys with a word-processing package, print the necessary number of copies, administer the surveys to prospective respondents, and input data by keyboard into a computerized database. Although the ability to automate data capture of survey information using scanning technology has been around since the 1960s, the cost of purchasing the hardware (scanner) and software has been prohibitive for smaller users (Dillman, 2000). In the past decade, advances in computer technology have made this a more cost-effective approach.

Currently, two types of optical scanning ("opscan") technologies are used in the field. Optical mark recognition (OMR) systems allow for reading the presence or absence of marks (usually small ovals or bubbles that are filled in by the respondent). OMR systems work by scanning a printed form, reading predefined positions, and recording where marks are made on the form. Optical character recognition (OCR) systems allow for reading handwritten text, numbers, and images (in addition to check marks and Xs). OCR creates a complete image of the document that is then imported into a computer, allowing for the electronic storage and retrieval of information (Dillman, 2000). Once questionnaires have been scanned and processed, a variety of software packages allow the data to be saved in formats that can be used with most data analysis packages (e.g., SPSS, Excel, Access). Both systems offer the advantage of gathering large amounts of data quickly and easily without the need for costly data entry time. They also offer a higher degree of accuracy than can be achieved through manual entry. In the past, one of the cited drawbacks to using OMR was the need for users to produce preprinted questionnaires or forms that typically entailed outsourcing the printing of the surveys. This process was often costly, inflexible, and incapable of meeting design change requirements at short notice. Progress in OMR now allows users to create and print their own forms (using ordinary word-processing software or more specialized software programs) and then use a scanner to read in the information (Bergeron, 1998). Various user-friendly software packages (e.g., Remark, Magenta, Form Storm, Vision OMR, SMS Storm) and inexpensive general-purpose scanners are available.

Researchers are encouraged to carefully examine the tasks they wish to undertake (e.g., scanning simple marks on papers such as test answer and ID numbers vs. pictures or handwritten characters) before deciding on which type of scanner and software package to purchase. Currently there are hundreds of scanners on the market, offering a variety of different features at prices that change constantly. Important features to consider include speed, price (under $1,000 to over $4,000), duplex capabilities (scanning two sides at once), automatic document feeder size, the size of the paper that can be scanned, and how the scanner will be used (volume of usage: occasional, regular, or heavy usage). Like scanners, software packages range in price depending on the number of users and the features offered. Due to space limitations, the advantages and disadvantages of each measurement type are not discussed in the text but are highlighted in exhibits. Exhibit 5.1 summarizes the advantages and disadvantages of using paper-and-pencil questionnaires.

Web Surveys

The 1990s brought a proliferation of Web-based survey companies that offer a large array of online survey software packages and services for conducting survey research (Wright, 2005). Although more scientific research

---

Exhibit 5.1

Advantages and Disadvantages of Paper-and-Pencil Questionnaires

Advantages

- Traditional format is familiar to schools.
- Format does not require technology and computer resources that may be less available in urban, rural, or depressed areas of the country.

Disadvantages

- Creation and administration are costly because of material and labor.
- Data entry is required (either manually or via scanner).
- Manual data entry is error prone.

---

has been devoted to Web-based surveys in recent years, no consensus has emerged as to whether response rates are similar or different between the Internet and more traditional paper-and-pencil modes of administration. Early studies indicated that response rates for Web-based surveys were poor (Archer, 2003; Truell, Bartlett, & Alexander, 2002), but more recent studies indicate better (Kiernan, Kiernan, Oyler, & Gilles, 2005) or no differences in response rates (Carini, Hayek, Kuh, Kennedy, & Ouimet, 2003) between traditional mail surveys and Web surveys. Response rates vary considerably among studies, reflecting differences in the methodology, the research problem being addressed, and the characteristics of the study population. Although no consensus has emerged, it is important for researchers to have a basic understanding of the current features and services available through Web survey software companies before evaluating whether a Web survey suits their needs.

Web surveys contain the same types of questions as those found on traditional paper-and-pencil questionnaires (Likert type, semantic differential, checklists, open-ended comment boxes), the only difference being that participants complete and submit the information over the Internet rather than returning the questionnaire in person or by mail. However, Web surveys offer different design features that are not possible with traditional paper-and-pencil surveys. These features include the use of multimedia (animation, video clips, audio, pictures), skip logic, popup instructions, drop-down menus, filter questions (to tailor surveys to individual characteristics of survey respondents), and an infinite variety of colors and shapes, which provide a level of technical sophistication and interaction between respondent and questionnaire that cannot be achieved with paper surveys. Attractive, professional-looking Web surveys are easy to create and manage utilizing any of the Web survey software packages that are commercially available.

Currently, two types of Web-based software tools are available for researchers who are interested in creating Web surveys. The first and most popular type involves the use of hosted survey software/computer programs that reside on a company's Web site. Researchers rent the survey software/programs that are housed on the company's server but are able to create and conduct the online surveys from their own computers. Advantages of this approach include no large upfront costs, quick implementation, information technology (IT) support services, and regular upgrades to the survey's functionality (Van Bennekom, 2007). The second, albeit less common, type involves the use of PC survey software that researchers are required to purchase from a Web survey company but that reside on their own desktop or server. Owning the software enables researchers to create multiple online surveys of any length as opposed to being charged per survey, per time period (e.g., by the month), by number of responses, by survey length, or a combination of these options. One disadvantage of owning software, however, is that customers have to pay for software upgrades, which typically become outdated relatively quickly given the rapid advances in software development (Wright, 2005).

Both types of Web survey software tools use some type of HTML (Hypertext Markup Language) online form to collect data. After completing an online survey, respondents click on a "submit" button that transmits the survey responses to the researchers. The Web software provides researchers with the ability to monitor the number of participants who have completed surveys in real time and to assess the completeness of their data (e.g., which items participants are skipping). Furthermore, these approaches enable researchers to conduct preliminary analyses with the data at any time by exporting survey responses to statistical software packages such SPSS and SAS.

Web survey companies offer a wide variety of services and software features. In general, companies typically offer different options for customer service support (e.g., e-mail support, phone support), online questionnaire features, and data-tracking and analysis features (e.g., tracking of survey respondent e-mail, e-mail response notification, real-time tracking of item responses, the ability to export survey responses to statistical software packages such as SAS and SPSS). Some companies offer a more expansive array of services for conducting online surveys, including the use of consultants to assist with creating Web surveys from scratch or from an existing paper-and-pencil survey, sampling and data collection services (e.g., conducting phone interviews, using company e-mail lists to generate samples, conducting online focus groups), and data analysis and interpretation services. We recommend that researchers interested in conducting Web surveys assess their research needs, budget, and research timeframe and comparison shop before deciding on which company to use. Exhibit 5.2 outlines the advantages and disadvantages of using Web surveys.

Interviews

In-person or phone interviews with students, teachers, and school personnel offer another rich source of information for researchers interested in conducting school-based research. This technique allows researchers to obtain quantitative information more reliably than paper-and-pencil questionnaires or Web surveys, in that they can make sure respondents understand the questions and reduce the number of questions respondents skip or mark incorrectly. However, quantitative data are not the only type of information gathered via interview techniques. Qualitative interviews are often conducted by staff members or research assistants trained to administer the interview utilizing a standardized interview protocol, with responses being recorded by audio- and/or video-recording equipment. Interviews

---

Exhibit 5.2

Advantages and Disadvantages of Web Surveys

Advantages

- Cost is lower (no paper, printing, postage, data entry, or labor costs).
- No data entry is required.
- Reliability is greater as there are no data-entry mistakes.
- Survey implementation time is reduced.
- Wider geographic areas can be covered.
- Ease of use is increased.
- Data turnaround is faster (can process and analyze data as they come in rather than having to wait for data entry and cleaning).
- Time of the researchers is saved.
- Design features that are not possible with paper-and-pencil surveys can be offered (e.g., multimedia, skip logic, pop-up instructions, filter questions, infinite number of colors and shapes).

Disadvantages

- Access to computer technology in school settings is required.
- Computer literacy of school staff is required.
- Additional security and confidentiality issues are raised.
- Problems can result due to the potential effects of differing computer equipment and telecommunication access.

---

are then transcribed verbatim either by a professional transcription service or by a research assistant utilizing a word-processing program. Data analysis typically involves examination of consistent themes in the data, which are then coded (and often quantified).

Although qualitative data analysis software programs (e.g., NUDIST, NVivo, Atlas/ti, Ethnography, MaxQD, HyperResearch, WinMax) have been available since the mid-1980s (Ozkan, 2004), their use by school-based researchers has been limited (Bourdon, 2002). Although these qualitative data analysis software programs offer researchers the potential to process qualitative data faster and more precisely, the user interface is often criticized for being difficult to use (Konig, n.d.), and the initial learning curve has been described as steep (LoPresti, 1997). Despite these criticisms, using qualitative data analysis programs for analyzing interview data offers researchers a means of improving methodological rigor.

Researchers conducting large-scale research projects in multiple locations should consider using computer-assisted telephone interviewing (CATI) systems rather than in-person interviewing to reduce the amount of money and staff needed to conduct high-quality interviews. CATI is an interactive computer system that allows interviewers to ask questions over the phone while sitting at their computer terminals. First, the interview is programmed into the computer, with most of the questions being in a multiple-choice format so that the interviewer needs only to point and click on the respondent's answer. Interviewers type the respondent's answers into the computer as the interview proceeds, thus eliminating the need for separate data entry. Answers are then translated into a code by the CATI system and exported to a database that is then used for data analysis. CATI leads to greater standardization of the interview by automatically controlling questionnaire branching, scheduling future calls, and capturing a variety of management information about the interview. We outline the advantages and disadvantages of interviews in Exhibit 5.3.

Archival Data

The use of archival data from schools—such as standardized test scores (achievement test data), report card data (e.g., grades), number of suspensions, number of absences, and special education referral rates—is a valuable source of information. Early on in the project, researchers interested in obtaining archival data from school systems should set up a meeting with school personnel (usually a school's research office or school record office) in charge of school records to discuss data availability (i.e., what types of data the researcher will be requesting and when the school system will make the data available). Researchers should be prepared before the meeting and visit the county's, district's, or school's Web site to see what test score data are typically available. When making requests to school dis-

---

Exhibit 5.3

Advantages and Disadvantages of Interviews

Advantages

- Researchers can make sure respondents understand questions.
- No items are missing.
- Rich contextual information about the school environment is provided for researchers evaluating intervention programs (e.g., types of programming, perceptions of challenges/successes of programs or of continuing needs).
- Researchers can better understand the unique perspectives of different stakeholders (e.g., teachers, students, principals, administrators) and the processes (e.g., mediators and moderators) that underlie school outcomes.

Disadvantages

- Interview process is expensive.
- Interview process is time consuming.
- Qualitative data analysis software programs for analyzing interview data may be difficult to use.

---

tricts, researchers should be as explicit as possible about the test data they are requesting (e.g., what academic subject or subjects, for which population or subpopulations of students, in which grades?) so that the school will know how much staff would need to be devoted to record retrieval. Researchers should be mindful that while the request for archival data does not involve teacher time, it does require school staff time to prepare the data files or copy paper files. Advances in computer technology have made it possible for many school systems to include electronic storage of archival test score data and grades. Although the capability is not widely available in all parts of the country or all school systems, the trend to archive data electronically will increase the collaborative opportunities between researchers and schools. We outline the advantages and disadvantages of using archival data in Exhibit 5.4.

Exhibit 5.4

Advantages and Disadvantages to Archival Data

Advantages

- No additional work is required from teachers, students, and administrators.
- No additional demands are placed on teachers or interfere with instructional time in the classroom.
- Standardized test score/achievement data are more objective than self-report data.

Disadvantages

- Test score data are not standardized and systematized across schools.
- Large amount of variability exists in the maintenance of school archival data (e.g., some schools keep paper-and-pencil copies of grades and achievement data, whereas others have converted to an electronic medium).
- Maintenance of school archival data is bound not only by policies and procedures of individual schools and school districts but also by the quality of the staff maintaining the school records.
- Grades have been criticized for being subjective because there is no uniform metric used among teachers across schools.
- Data analysis can be complicated when different schools in the same district utilize different standardized tests and may require statistical consultation from experts.

In the era of the No Child Left Behind Act (NCLB), pressure has increased on schools and teachers to provide evidence that what they are doing inside the classroom (e.g., particular interventions, teaching strategies) translates into improved academic achievement for students. Researchers who offer to analyze such test score data are actually assisting with fulfilling one of the mandates of NCLB, namely, to document that adequate yearly progress is being made by all students. School personnel may find the proposals of researchers more relevant to their own situations if researchers can clearly articulate the link between the study's research question and the school's need for the same information to fulfill NCLB requirements.

CASE EXAMPLE: DEVELOPING, INSTITUTING, AND REFINING WEB SURVEY–BASED MEASUREMENT IN A LARGE-SCALE RESEARCH PROJECT

The second half of this chapter provides a case example of a university–school collaboration that utilized Web survey technology to conduct a randomized control intervention trial in 45 elementary schools within a Virginia school district. The goal of the intervention trial was to determine the effectiveness of Instructional Consultation Teams, which are a comprehensive teacher intervention package consisting of interdisciplinary teams, collaborative consultation, and an evaluation/implementation package to enhance teacher competence in addressing academic and behavioral concerns in struggling learners (Rosenfield et al., 2008). The case example illustrates the process of choosing a measurement protocol, the real-world communication and technical challenges that occurred after measurement decisions were made, and how researchers and school staff used feedback to make adjustments to the chosen measures.

The process of developing the measures began with an extensive review of the literature to identify existing measures in the following domains of interest: student achievement and social–emotional functioning and perceptions by teachers of their efficacy, instructional practices, job satisfaction, and school climate. Measures were obtained using traditional library research methods/search engines (i.e., PsycINFO, ERIC); also, researchers corresponded directly with authors via e-mail to obtain permissions to use measures and to locate measures that were difficult to find. After a careful review of the measures, a decision was made to primarily utilize and adapt existing measures that possessed sound psychometric properties and that mapped onto the constructs of interest. Use of existing measures would allow for comparisons with other studies and would also save time and resources. To reduce the burden for teachers of completing lengthy survey questionnaires, the research team shortened existing measures and simplified their wording according to Dillman's (2000) techniques for writing good survey questions.

In the case of teacher instructional practices, where the research team felt that no existing measure adequately tapped the construct of interest, the team developed and piloted their own measure. Two teacher survey instruments were developed and shared with the school district: a 100-item Teacher Self-Report Survey (TSRS) and a 36-item Teacher Report on Student Behavior Survey (TRSBS).

As an outcome of conversations with school-district personnel, it was decided that the surveys would be administered electronically rather than via the more traditional paper-and-pencil mode. Given the magnitude of the data collection endeavor (collecting data on over 1,900 teachers and 27,700 students in 45 different schools that were spread out across a large county) and the district's positive experience with the use of electronic technology to administer surveys in the past, it was felt that electronic surveys would be a more cost-effective and faster way to distribute surveys, eliminating the costs associated with postage, paper, data entry, and labor for survey administration. In addition, it would allow for real-time monitoring of data collection activities, be less prone to data-entry errors, and allow for faster analysis of results.

As part of the collaboration, the university and the district divided ownership and responsibility for the administration of the two surveys. The district was responsible for the online data collection through which teachers completed reports on all of their students (the TRSBS). The district took on this part of the study as a way to protect student information and so that they would have access to the results. To reduce the burdens on teachers, a grant supported resources to free the teachers to complete the surveys. The school district's IT department worked with its Office of Program Evaluation to develop an interactive, intranet-based survey interface that allowed teachers to access their student roster list and to electronically enter data for each student in their class.

In the case of the second survey, the University of Maryland (UMD) collaborators were responsible for the online administration of the TSRS.

Because of time and resource constraints, the UMD research team decided to develop the Web survey after conducting a comprehensive investigation of the various Web survey companies and identifying the features that were most important for the research project (e.g., ease of use, security, cost).

To achieve the highest response rate possible for completion of the Web survey, the university research team adapted Dillman's system of utilizing five compatible contacts (see Dillman's [2000] discussion of Tailored Design Method), which has been used to maximize response in mail surveys. Adaptations for the present study included the following. First, a schoolwide principals' meeting was held prior to the start of data collection, during which the university research team and the district program evaluation staff informed principals in both intervention and control schools about the upcoming surveys. Second, after the meeting, principals were expected to inform their staff about the data collection procedures, and the university research team sent a prenotice letter and small incentive (a notepad) to teachers approximately 1 week prior to data collection. Third, a link to the survey was sent to teachers via e-mail with directions. And, finally, four follow-up/thank-you e-mails were sent that also contained directions for completing the survey.

During the 1st year, server problems in the district slowed down the ability of teachers to respond to the TRSBS. To achieve the highest possible response rate, the Office of Program Evaluation contacted schools with low completion rates (under 60%) and offered them a paper-and-pencil version. This improved response rates from an initial 76% to 83%. The final Year 1 response rate for the TSRS was 88% (85% treatment, 90% control) and 83% for the TRSBS (81% treatment, 88% control).

LESSONS LEARNED

In this section, we discuss the lessons learned from using the Web survey technology in the present school-based research project from two perspectives: the school district and the researcher.

School District Perspective

From the school district perspective, many communication and techno-logical challenges were experienced during Year 1, which led to additional communication efforts and revisions to the Internet data collection proce-dures during Year 2. The challenges, solutions, and lessons learned regard-ing measurement are addressed next.

Communication Challenges

Although the university and the district provided principals and teachers with information about the study and the surveys ahead of time, it became apparent that better communication with schools was needed earlier on in the life of the project to clearly articulate expectations regarding the Web and intranet surveys to schools and teachers.

- Schools, particularly the control schools, did not receive enough infor-mation early on about the study, which led to confusion and frustra-tion during the data collection process. While treatment schools began receiving training for their IC-team facilitator and administrators in summer/fall 2005, control schools did not receive much information. University researchers presented briefly at a principals' meeting that took place close to the outset of the initial round of data collection. This presentation had been slated to occur earlier but was rescheduled because of a weather-related closing. As a result, principals, especially at the control schools, did not have a great deal of up front information for their teachers about the data collection activities that were to take place. Treatment schools had the advantage of having IC-team facilita-tors at their schools to explain the study to their teachers, while no such "experts" at the control schools existed.

- The Office of Program Evaluation was inundated with phone calls and e-mails about the study during the 3 weeks of data collection. Given that the office only had a few staff members, the study overwhelmed the other functions and efforts of the office during that time frame. Although many of the inquiries from teachers were related to the tech-nical problems they were experiencing (see Technological Challenges below), other questions were about the purpose of the study and the difference between the two survey instruments.

Communication Solutions

At the end of Year 1, the school district and the university research team held a research meeting that led to the following solutions being put into place in Year 2:

- The Office of Program Evaluation worked more closely with the university research team to facilitate introductory sessions for principals before data collection began. At these sessions, university researchers described the study in more detail, the impact of missing data was discussed, plans for information dissemination and data collection were clearly articulated, and administrators were given the opportunity to ask questions.
- The university provided a research assistant to the district for the duration of the data collection window. This research assistant fielded phone calls from schools and calculated school- and teacher-level response rates throughout the process, thereby greatly reducing the burden felt by the Office of Program Evaluation in Year 1.
- The school district's IT department provided the Office of Program Evaluation with a link to view real-time completion numbers by teachers, which made the response rate calculations easier to conduct in a timely fashion. This enabled the Office of Program Evaluation to tell a teacher right away how many students were showing as complete, which reduced anxiety for teachers who were eager to do a good job.

Overall, these communication and technological solutions came out of a feedback-driven model of working collaboratively with schools. This model involved utilizing data (e.g., response rate information) and feedback from school district staff to improve and refine the initial measurement decisions made in Year 1 (namely to use Web survey technology rather than the traditional surveys). When problems arose, instead of changing the measurement approach, the research team worked collaboratively to develop solutions and to implement them in Year 2. This approach enabled researchers and school staff to benefit maximally from the measurement decisions that were made at the beginning of the research collaboration.

Technological Challenges

The school district's administration of the TRSBS was hindered by the following technological challenges:

- The number of teachers accessing the site at the same time created severe network slowness in some schools, and the fact that many schools were running on old, and thus slow, servers further complicated this problem. The process of completing the TRSBS, which should have taken only a few minutes per student, took teachers much longer because of these network issues.
- Weather closures disabled the servers completely at some of the schools.

Technological Solutions

- In Year 1, the technical problems were severe enough to warrant the development of a paper-and-pencil version of the TRSBS, which was distributed to schools that experienced network disruptions.
- In Year 2, the window for data collection was divided across the district's administrative areas (with different areas going at different times) to reduce server overload and the number of schools affected at a given time.
- Improvements in the district's infrastructure resulted in the IT department placing the intranet-based TRSBS on a newer, faster server, which reduced survey completion time. As a result, data collection went more smoothly, as demonstrated in dramatically increased response rates on the TRSBS (83% in Year 1 to 94% in Year 2, with no school under 80%).

Researcher Perspective

From a researcher perspective, the Web survey technology provided an extremely cost-efficient, user-friendly way to conduct large-scale survey research. The only drawbacks to the selected Web survey provider's features

were its inability to handle respondents logging off the survey and returning at a later time and its inability to disallow duplicate identification numbers (rules for deleting duplicates were created). Overall, the research team
was pleased with the professional appearance of the survey, the reliability
of the technology (no slowness or server crashes), the ability for real-time
viewing of the status of data collection (easy to figure out how many
respondents had not completed the surveys), and the ease with which the
data could be exported to Excel and then transported to SPSS for data
analysis.

In contrast to the ease of the university's Web survey administration,
the school district's administration of the TRSBS via the intranet was more
hindered by technological difficulties in Year 1. Although many of the challenges were remedied in Year 2, one of the lessons learned for researchers
conducting school-based research projects is to pilot any and all computer
technology ahead of time with multiple users simultaneously (if that is how
the measures are to be delivered), if possible. Overall, it is important for
researchers who are considering the use of Internet technology to collect
data to be aware of the technological challenges that can emerge and to try
to anticipate problems and work out solutions ahead of time.

REFERENCES

Archer, T. M. (2003). Web-based surveys. *Journal of Extension, 41*(4), 1–5.
Bergeron, B. P. (1998, August). Optical mark recognition: Tallying information
from filled-in bubbles. *Postgraduate Medicine, 104*(2). Retrieved January 22,
2008, from http://www.postgradmed.com/issues/1998/08_98/dd_aug.htm
Bourdon, S. (2002, May). The integration of qualitative data analysis software
in research strategies: Resistances and possibilities. *Forum Qualitative Social
Research, 3*(2). Retrieved January 22, 2008, from http://www.qualitative-
research.net/fqs-texte/2-02/2-02bourdon-e.htm
Carini, R. M., Hayek, J. C., Kuh, G. D., Kennedy, J. M., & Ouimet, J. A. (2003). Col-
lege student responses to Web and paper surveys: Does mode matter? *Research
in Higher Education, 44*, 1–19.
Dillman, D. A. (2000). *Mail and Internet surveys: The Tailored Design Method.* New
York: Wiley.
Kiernan, N. E., Kiernan, M., Oyler, M. A., & Gilles, C. (2005). Is a Web survey as
effective as a mail survey? A field experiment among computer users. *American
Journal of Evaluation, 26*, 245–252.

Konig, T. (n.d.). *CAQDAS: A primer.* Retrieved January 25, 2008, from http://www.lboro.ac.uk/rsearch/mmethods/research/software/caqdas_primer.html

LoPresti, F. (1997, Summer). Exploring NUD-IST for qualitative analysis. *Statistics and Social Sciences.* Retrieved January 25, 2008, from http://www.nyu.edu/its/pubs/connect/archives/97summer/loprestinudist.html

Ozkan, B. C. (2004). Using Nvivo to analyze qualitative classroom data on constructivist learning environments. *Qualitative Report, 9,* 589–603.

Rosenfield, S., Silva, A., & Gravois, T. (2008). Bringing instructional consultation to scale: Research and development of IC and IC teams. In W. P. Erchul & S. M. Sheridan (Eds.), *Handbook of research in school consultation: Empirical foundations for the field* (pp. 203–223). Hillsdale, NJ: Erlbaum.

Shadish, W. R., Cook, T. D., & Campbell, D. T. (2002). *Experimental and quasi-experimental designs for general causal inference.* Boston: Houghton Mifflin.

Truell, A. D., Bartlett, J. E., & Alexander, M. W. (2002). Response rate, speed, and completeness: A comparison of Internet-based and mail surveys. *Behavior Research Methods, Instruments, and Computers, 34,* 50–54.

Van Bennekom, F. V. (2007, January). Tips for selecting an online survey software tools. *Service Insights Newsletter.* Retrieved July 21, 2008, from http://www.greatbrook.com/online_survey_tools.htm

Wright, K. B. (2005). Researching Internet-based populations: Advantages and disadvantages of online survey research, online questionnaire authoring software packages, and Web survey services. *Journal of Computer-Mediated Communication, 10*(3). Retrieved July 21, 2008, from http://jcmc.indiana.edu/vol10/issue3/wright.html

6

Implementation Quality in School-Based Research: Roles for the Prevention Researcher

Heather K. Warren, Celene E. Domitrovich, and Mark T. Greenberg

The challenge of bridging science and theory with policy and practice exists in many disciplines. When interventions are replicated in communities, they are conducted with lower quality than when they were originally tested under controlled conditions (Durlak & DuPre, 2008; Fixsen, Naoom, Blase, Friedman, & Wallace, 2005; Rohrbach, Grana, Sussman, & Valente, 2006). The National Institutes of Health's Roadmap for Medical Research refers to this challenge as one of two "translational roadblocks" in the research enterprise and calls for an emphasis on "Type 2 translational research" to understand and provide solutions that facilitate the transfer process involved in widespread dissemination (Woolf, 2008). As reflected in the No Child Left Behind legislation, the government is mandating the use of evidence-based interventions (EBIs) to ensure children and families are receiving programs of high quality shown to "work." The proliferation of EBIs within the contemporary climate of accountability creates substantial opportunities for schools to implement comprehensive programming to meet the complex needs of their students.

Because schools are increasingly invested in using EBIs in preventing a variety of outcomes, including behavioral disorders, poor school achievement, and early substance use and abuse, it follows that there is heightened interest in monitoring the quality with which these interventions are imple-

The authors would like to thank Elise Cappella and Patricia Graczyk for their helpful comments on earlier versions of the manuscript. Support for this chapter was received from National Institute of Child Health and Human Development Grant 5 R01 HD 51514-03.

mented (Berryhill & Prinz, 2003; Catalano, Berglund, Ryan, Lonczak, & Hawkins, 2002; Greenberg, Domitrovich, & Bumbarger, 2005; Hahn et al., 2007; Ramey, Ramey, & Lanzi, 2006). Furthermore, understanding the factors that influence the quality of implementation is essential to provide guidelines and policies that can improve program implementation because higher quality is consistently related to more positive outcomes (Durlak & DuPre, 2008). Given the current climate in education and the current focus in prevention research, school-based practitioners and prevention researchers are likely to find common ground with respect to issues of implementation quality.

A central challenge to prevention research is determining what factors influence the ability of schools to implement programs and policies with a similar degree of fidelity as when they were first scientifically evaluated. As schools engage in the enterprise of program utilization to meet the demands of current legislation, prevention research can realize maximized returns by initiating more collaborative approaches to program implementation and evaluation. In this chapter, we describe the potential for developing collaborative processes between prevention scientists and school-based practitioners that can improve implementation, as well as provide researchers with essential information for improving implementation and intervention processes. In doing so, we present a model for conceptualizing the monitoring of the implementation of school-based programs. The goal of this chapter is to help those interested in implementing empirically based programs to maximize the program's potential for successful outcomes while creating long-term, mutually beneficial partnerships between schools and researchers.

INTEGRATING COLLABORATIVE APPROACHES AND PREVENTION SCIENCE IN PROGRAM EVALUATION

A decade ago, Weissberg and Greenberg (1998) identified the benefits of integrating the divergent approaches of collaborative community research and prevention science paradigms in the program evaluation process. A key strength of this integration is the marrying of researchers' theoretical and methodological expertise with the practitioners' real-world knowledge and experiences with the program and the intervention delivery setting. Taken together, these research perspectives allow school-based researchers to achieve the best of both worlds utilizing two perspectives that differ in theory, research, and evidence. The integration of these two perspectives has the potential to benefit both researchers and practitioners, but it is not without challenges.

Collaborative Community Research Paradigm

Collaborative researchers recognize the school or community as an integral part of the program's success. From the outset, they engage the users, beneficiaries, and stakeholders of a program in the research process and, using their local knowledge, gather a portrait of the problem in context (Wandersman, 2003). This includes an analysis of the community needs, issues, and resources, as well as an assessment of the risk and protective factors present in the population. This research tradition also emphasizes the setting's capacity for creating infrastructure to support interventions (Elias & Tobias, 1996). A genuine collaborative approach begins with community values and perspectives and uses researchers as facilitators such that the integration of the intervention model occurs within the community rather than on the community. This results in a rich process knowledge of the intervention as it operates within the context. In these situations, intended users of interventions may be more committed to using the research findings because they have been involved in the dissemination process and feel it reflects their particular experience.

Prevention Science Paradigm

Prevention researchers develop interventions on the basis of developmental epidemiological data (Kellam, Koretz, & Moscicki, 1999) and use experimental methods of research to determine whether interventions are effective at reducing the prevalence and incidence of problems at a population level. They are guided by the prevention research cycle elaborated by Mrazek and Haggerty (1994) in their report for the Institute of Medicine

(IOM). The cycle describes the stages of research that are necessary to develop, test, and disseminate interventions.

A primary tenet of the IOM report is that programs should not be widely disseminated without documented efficacy. This necessitates testing the intervention using a controlled design, such as the gold standard of evaluation known as the *randomized clinical trial* (RCT). These formal evaluations, *efficacy trials,* establish whether an intervention is capable of significantly changing targeted outcomes for participants who receive the program, as compared with those who do not (Flay et al., 2005). Depending on the origin of the intervention, efficacy trials are sometimes conducted in academic settings. In these situations, efficacy trials are followed by studies that determine how the intervention operates under conditions of local ownership (*effectiveness trials*). These trials mark a shift from asking whether interventions work to asking under what conditions are interventions most effective and how those conditions can be created. Because of the proliferation of EBIs and the demand for their use in community settings, the field of prevention science is increasingly focused on conducting effectiveness trials and research on the process of taking EBIs to scale by distributing them more widely (*dissemination*). As such, the need to address contextual considerations is becoming more evident (see also chap. 8, this volume). Program developers are finding that it is not always easy to integrate interventions into community institutions such as schools. Programs are not consistently implemented with quality and are difficult to sustain (Elliott & Mihalic, 2004). For additional discussion about efficacy and effectiveness of interventions, see chapter 3 in this volume.

An Integrated Approach

The reprioritization of contextual relevance into the traditional prevention science paradigm can be addressed by incorporating community-oriented perspectives. As Weissberg and Greenberg (1998) suggested, hybrid community-centered models enable communities to use EBIs more effectively because the community partners' (users, beneficiaries, stakeholders) unique knowledge of problem, targeted outcome, and unique insight on ways to support and maintain the intervention is taken into account (Wandersman, 2003). When community members, practitioners, and others directly affected by the intervention program partner with researchers, they may generate intervention and support system models that may be more likely to overcome these implementation and dissemination challenges.

In some cases, unacceptable implementation drift occurs because practitioners modify the intervention. Although this may increase acceptability, utilization, or sustainability, it results in delivery that diverges from the original program model. Applied scientists have to be aware that when moving from carefully controlled trials to dissemination, populations and settings vary widely. Practitioners may need to adjust EBIs to fit the social, cultural, or structural conditions of the context. As Castro, Barrera, and Martinez (2004) indicated, fitting the program to the community, on the one hand, and maintaining its original fidelity, on the other, is challenging.

A CONCEPTUAL MODEL OF IMPLEMENTATION QUALITY

The importance of monitoring implementation quality has been discussed across a number of disciplines, including education, psychology, and public health. Prior to the 1990s, it was common for evaluations to focus primarily on measuring target outcomes. They were referred to as "black box" evaluations because they provided little information regarding why a program was effective or how it could be improved (Patton, 1979). As such, process-level inquiry was largely absent from evaluation research. In contrast, a theory-driven approach to evaluation specifies principles, practices, and programs that are linked through a causal mechanism to specified, intended outcomes. Chen (1998, 2003) called attention to the system that supports the intervention in his version of a theory-driven evaluation. In addition to a causal theory, Chen proposed a prescriptive theory that describes the means and the context that are needed for the intervention to be implemented effectively and that must be specified and used to guide evaluation. These two conceptually distinct components—the intervention and its corresponding support system—must be considered in assessing the quality of implementation (Chen, 1998; Greenberg, Domitrovich, Graczyk, & Zins, 1999). This conceptualization of implementation extends traditional perspectives that focused solely on fidelity to the intervention components (Moncher & Prinz, 1991). Implementation quality is the discrepancy between what is planned and what is delivered. To assess quality, the planned model for each of these components must be specified and monitored to determine the standard against which the actual program that is conducted will be compared.

Intervention

A theory-driven approach to intervention results in the identification of a set of core components or elements that are believed to be the active ingredients of the intervention based on the theorized mechanism of change (McNeal, Hansen, Harrington, & Giles, 2004; Skara, Rohrbach, Sun, & Sussman, 2005). These features or practices must be implemented well for the intervention to be effective. Absence of core components, poorly delivered core components, or poorly managed adaptations of core components may result in failed implementation. However, if the measures of implementation are specifically aligned with the hypothesized core elements of the program, data on the occurrence, quality, and adaptation of practices can provide much needed information about whether and which of the hypothesized program elements are necessary to obtain positive program outcomes, as well as information about the effect of program adaptation on program outcomes. This facilitates the distinction between core elements and adaptable characteristics of the intervention. With respect to school-based research, there is considerable evidence that teachers routinely adapt programs (Datnow & Castellano, 2000; Ringwalt et al., 2003). Yet, to date, little contemporary research has focused on the impact of the adaptations on program outcomes.

Support System

Regardless of the program's specific content or delivery, effective implementation requires a system of support, and quality is higher when implementers are provided training on the knowledge and skills needed to conduct the intervention (McCormick, Steckler, & McLeroy, 1995). Research suggests that training should be ongoing and provide opportunities for trainees' active engagement (Putnam & Borko, 2000). This type of training, often referred to as coaching or mentoring, facilitates the implementation process by helping users understand the intervention, the mechanics of program delivery, and appropriate ways to tailor, adapt, and integrate the intervention with existing practices (Dusenbury et al., 2007). Although there are exceptions, few studies have evaluated different training models to determine what content, structure, or practices are the most essential for preparing implementers (see, e.g., Basen-Engquist et al., 1994). Again, this means that schools have little empirical information on which to base any deviations from the original support system model.

Effective support systems extend beyond the individuals delivering the intervention and include the infrastructure necessary to coordinate the deployment of the intervention (Greenberg et al., 1999). Research on the implementation of school-based interventions suggests that principals should be considered a part of this system in educational settings. Principals' authority and control over resources enable the creation of supportive work environments, facilitating effective use of innovations by teachers and staff (Kam, Greenberg, & Walls, 2003). Additional work on the mechanisms through which administrative leaders facilitate implementation is required before their role can be included as a formal part of the support system model, however.

MEASURING IMPLEMENTATION QUALITY

Poor implementation quality, whether in the context of a research trial or service setting, is a major factor underlying the failure of an intervention to produce desired effects (Derzon, Sale, Springer, & Brounstein, 2005). Despite this, implementation quality is often not monitored adequately in research trials or community replications. A strong assessment of the discrepancy between the "model" version of the intervention and the support system (as conceived by the developers) and its implementation in real-world settings by school system personnel should include multiple indicators of program adherence. Comprehensive measurement of the quality of the implementation of the intervention and the support system should include assessments of adherence in terms of *fidelity* (degree to which an intervention and its support system are conducted as planned), *dosage* (specific units of an intervention and support system), and *quality of delivery* (engagement, sensitivity, and responsiveness; Dane & Schneider, 1998; Dusenbury, Brannigan, & Hansen, 2005; see also chap. 7, this volume), as well as assessing the quality of training and ongoing technical assistance.

Determination of the intervention's fidelity is commonly assessed via implementer self-report or observation, or by having participants report on the occurrence of core elements (i.e., whether specific content was delivered or the techniques used). Support systems can be assessed in a similar fashion. Dosage can be quantified in terms of specific units of an intervention (e.g., number of lessons delivered) or amount of time that a participant is exposed to an intervention (e.g., hours of contact). Dosage of the implementation support model is similarly quantified via the number of hours of training or the number of contacts from a coach or supervisor (Payne, Gottfredson, & Gottfredson, 2006). Quality of delivery should be monitored by measuring implementers' knowledge of the intervention model and their skills (e.g., technical, interpersonal) in creating the appropriate learning context (see Dusenbury et al., 2005).

We wish to highlight not only the importance of ensuring high-quality implementation in school settings but also that of monitoring the ongoing implementation process both for contemporary researchers and practitioners. As communities take EBIs to scale, information regarding ongoing implementation quality provides the basis of an ongoing partnership between researchers and schools to promote positive outcomes while facilitating both the shared and unique objectives of each partner.

SUPPORTING SCHOOLS IN THE USE OF EVIDENCE-BASED INTERVENTIONS

Given the current educational climate, an increasingly common situation is the collaboration between schools and researchers created by a community initiative to implement EBIs. In these situations, schools or agencies have the resources (either through general funds or a grant) to conduct interventions, and they approach researchers for advice regarding which interventions to adopt, how to successfully conduct an intervention, or how to obtain their support in conducting an evaluation. In any of these situations, the ultimate goal is to implement an intervention with quality in order to change a targeted student outcome. This process begins with adequate preplanning and then involves a phase of implementation that requires monitoring and feedback to be successful. Depending on circumstances, an evaluation might also be included.

Preplanning

Any preparation by a school prior to conducting an intervention is considered preplanning. Research suggests there are characteristics related to the intervention and the immediate training/support system that foster high-quality implementation. These include program content based on a well-articulated theory of change (Tobler et al., 2000; Wilson, Gottfredson, & Najaka, 2001), the right fit between the program and the needs of the setting, and high-quality materials, including program standardization (Gottfredson & Gottfredson, 2002; Payne et al., 2006). All of these factors should be considered during the time when schools are considering interventions to adopt. If done well, preplanning increases the likelihood of high-quality implementation within a system (Graczyk, Domitrovich, Small, & Zins, 2006). The two critical stages of preplanning are choosing the right program and preparing the system for program use.

The successful implementation of an EBI begins with the choice of an appropriate strategy that targets identified needs. This choice depends on an accurate needs assessment and an accurate causative theory of how the problem develops and is maintained. One of the most important defining features of high-quality preventive interventions is their theoretical basis. The IOM preventive intervention research cycle (Mrazek & Haggerty, 1994) facilitates the development of theory-based interventions by specifying the use of epidemiological and longitudinal data to articulate etiological models of how problems develop and for identifying the specific risk and protective factors involved in this process. Interventions that are designed to target the malleable risk and protective factors are then considered theory based. Theory is confirmed when an intervention has a positive impact on targeted outcomes in a rigorous research study. If a community does not understand the theory of development underlying the problem they are targeting, they may choose the wrong intervention. Researchers can play an integral role as a resource to schools in the program selection process by assisting them with identification of their specific needs and suggesting theory-based interventions targeting those needs.

Empirical research suggests that implementers' perceptions and behavior prior to program adoption can influence implementation quality and commitment to an intervention (Han & Weiss, 2005). Implementers need to feel that the core principles underlying the intervention are consistent with their philosophy of what is acceptable when it comes to managing student behavior or improving their socioemotional functioning (Kealey, Peterson, Gaul, & Dinh, 2000; Rohrbach, Graham, & Hansen, 1993). It is also important that they perceive the program to be better than the current practice, feasible given current demands, and compatible with the values of the institution (Gottfredson & Gottfredson, 2002; Mihalic, Irwin, Fagan, Ballard, & Elliot, 2004; Ringwalt et al., 2003; Rogers, 2003). Some EBIs suggest that a level of endorsement from school staff (e.g., 80%) should be obtained before embarking on program implementation (Battistich, Schaps, Watson, Solomon, & Lewis, 2000). Acceptability can be increased when implementers are exposed to model implementers or exemplars of quality implementation in contextually similar schools. Sometimes this can be done by taking a small group of teachers to another school to observe the intervention or showing videotape footage of program implementation in similar settings. Researchers' expertise and experience utilizing programs is an asset to schools when they can demonstrate previous high-quality utilizations of the program to potential implementers early in the adoption phase to promote endorsement and buy-in.

In addition, an awareness of the need for an intervention, incentive for change, and involvement in the program adoption process by implementers can facilitate high-quality implementation (McCormick et al., 1995; Mihalic et al., 2004). Often decisions about innovations in schools are decided at the administrative level without staff input. Sharing community data that reflect the problem targeted by the EBI will promote early involvement. Explaining the purpose and goals of the initiative will facilitate implementers in becoming collaborators, rather than recipients, of the EBI. Similarly, providing an overview of the intervention logic model and allowing implementers to collaborate in planning has the potential to reduce resistance and promote high-quality implementation.

The quality of the programming materials may also influence the extent to which the program is received by its intended users. Implementers will return to these materials as a resource when they are confused or in need of guidance; therefore, these materials have great potential in promoting a clear, coherent, and consistent message about the implementation of a given program. They provide guidance and structure for the program and support the implementation team's knowledge of the program's content beyond that of any initial training experiences. The materials should therefore match the age, education, and cultural background of the target population. The visual appeal of the materials may also influence their perceived usability. Including implementers in the process of reviewing potential programs for the above characteristics will enhance their sense of involvement and control over the adoption process. Finally, program standardization is positively related to implementation quality (Payne et al., 2006). It involves the specification or documentation of the core components of an intervention. This is typically achieved by creating detailed instructional manuals and lesson plans. Most of the EBIs being endorsed by federal and state funding agencies are required to have these types of materials.

Preparing the System for Program Use

In addition to conducting a needs assessment and selecting the appropriate intervention, preplanning includes preparing the system for conducting the intervention. This includes training implementers and ensuring adequate support for the intervention. At minimum, implementers need to be prepared to effectively deliver the core content of the intervention (Fixsen et al., 2005). This includes adequate background knowledge regarding the intervention theory and instructional skills that are necessary to conduct the intervention. Knowledge of program theory allows implementers to understand the value of fidelity to the intervention components and reduces adaptations that might undermine intervention effectiveness.

The existing literature suggests that teachers struggle to implement evidence-based practices without ongoing supervision and support (Allison, Silverman, & Dignam, 1990; Dusenbury et al., 2007; Parcel et al., 2003; Penuel, Fishman, Yamaguchi, & Gallagher, 2007; Perry, Murray, & Griffin, 1990). A training and consultation phase long enough to ensure a thorough and working knowledge of the core program principles, and their translation into practice, is essential (Rose & Church, 1998). Joyce and Showers (2002) found that teachers provided with typical in-service training had the lowest levels of strategy implementation in the classroom, followed by teachers who received training that incorporated practice and feedback. The teachers with the highest levels of implementation were those who received training that included practice, feedback, and ongoing coaching and consultation. However, even with high levels of ongoing support, a proportion of teachers continued to exhibit low levels of implementation.

A strong leader who advocates using evidence-based practices within a school can have a significant impact on the successful implementation of interventions (Hallinger & Heck, 1996). Indeed, implementers' perceptions of administrative support are associated with high-quality implementation (Payne et al., 2006; Rohrbach, Ringwalt, Ennett, & Vincus, 2005). Effective administrators provide the oversight and accountability that are necessary to maintain focus and ensure follow-through by implementers in the schools (Rohrbach et al., 1993). They have the authority to specify program participation in staff job descriptions (Barrett, Bradshaw, & Lewis-Palmer, 2008) or require staff to allocate class time to implement the program. Administrators can also support communication and coordination among implementers to increase implementation effectiveness. Preplanning can be used to facilitate administrative support (both actual and perceived) by creating opportunities for building leaders to communicate expectations clearly (Corboy & McDonald, 2007).

For instance, our research indicated that the support and leadership of principals in school-based programming made substantial differences in the effectiveness of EBI program outcomes in inner-city public schools

(Kam et al., 2003). Presenting these research findings to district staff has facilitated interactions with building administration in establishing leadership roles for principals to promote high-quality outcomes for the children involved in the program. With this top-level support from the schools, the evidence-based program is likely to be more effective. Future dissemination efforts should consider the significance of principal support and leadership for programming initiatives in school-based initiatives.

MONITORING IMPLEMENTATION AND PROVIDING FEEDBACK

A process-level approach to implementation monitoring and evaluation is essential for improving the quality of implementation. Prevention researchers can facilitate these improvements by establishing collaborations that encourage dialogue and feedback between themselves and the practitioners, stakeholders, and beneficiaries of EBIs in schools and communities. To best support schools in their use of EBIs, we propose that from the onset of EBI adoption and throughout the intervention's utilization, a clearly articulated cyclical implementation feedback loop between researcher and practitioner must be established to achieve the mutual goal of continuous quality improvement. Implementation can be measured at several levels (e.g., student, classroom), and each of these levels has a different utility. While student level information might be useful at the analysis stage, it may be overwhelming as feedback regarding implementation. In contrast, classroom level feedback on teacher's quality of implementation is very useful for the feedback cycle between researcher and practitioner. The Collaborative for Academic, Social and Emotional Learning has created a developmental model that helps to support schools (or districts) through a multiyear process to ensure high-quality implementation and sustainability of EBIs (Devaney, O'Brien, Resnik, Keister, & Weissberg, 2006). This model assists schools in building a vision and identifying needs, through program selection, implementation, evaluation, and finally sustainable training and use. As previously outlined, this feedback process begins by defining the essential content and activities of the intervention and the support system and measuring the fidelity, dosage, and quality of delivery across both these components. If, for example, a school decided to implement a universal, teacher-taught, drug prevention curriculum, monitoring should begin with the training provided to teachers. This might include tracking who received training, teacher satisfaction with the training, and teacher efficacy to implement the curriculum.

After training, the implementation monitoring shifts to the intervention. This might involve collection of teacher "lesson logs" to track dosage, or quarterly observations by a consultant to assess quality of delivery or fidelity. Numerous options are available; the strategy used depends on time and available resources. During the implementation phase, it is important to also monitor the ongoing support system. At a minimum, this involves assessing administrative support (either directly or through implementer perceptions) and, if provided, coaching. Assessments of coaching might include the dosage (e.g., hours of contact) or the quality of the coach–implementer relationship. Including performance feedback in this process has been shown to improve implementation quality (Noell et al., 2005).

Regardless of the form, feedback focuses on the common goal of attending to quality of implementation of EBIs and provides essential feedback to stakeholders and researchers alike, facilitating decision making on the implementation process and, ultimately, student outcomes. With the mutual goal of responding to identified needs, the community and the researcher are reciprocally empowered as they progress through the constant monitoring of an EBI.

The course of action we propose is neither a single iteration nor a unidirectional feedback system. The process of quality implementation in naturalistic contexts requires ongoing monitoring and continual feedback from preplanning through sustainability efforts. Much of the literature describing successful collaborations around this process takes place over years (Elliott & Mihalic, 2004; Romanz, Kantor, & Elias, 2003). The application of an action research model involving an ongoing cycle of feedback such as we are suggesting is also unique in each community. Although undergoing this successive monitoring process may be an organic and community-specific enterprise, school-based researchers have a growing literature of research on implementation to begin hypothesizing action steps.

The most immediate and easy factors to address may be those related to the training or support system. For example, providing a booster training or additional support from a coach could be sufficient to raise implementation quality. This is an appropriate strategy if the problem is teacher competency. However, quality often suffers for reasons that are more challenging to address, such as implementer buy-in or systemic problems at the school building level.

Some schools have found that adequate buy-in at the top level may not necessarily be defined only in terms of administrator support. Strong local coordinators, key opinion leaders, or local "champions" for program success have also been predictive of the level of implementation in various school-based settings (Atkins, Graczyk, & Frazier, 2006; Fagan & Mihalic, 2003; Mihalic et al., 2004). These findings suggest that successful integration into the adopting agency (i.e., schools) may sometimes require the identification of key individuals, playing to their strengths within the context of interest, and supporting the system's adoption and adaptation of the program to enhance its effectiveness.

In addition to individual factors, there may also be more immediate contextual issues affecting implementation quality, such as classroom composition. High levels of student misconduct in the classroom can undermine teachers' self-efficacy with respect to behavior management and their perceptions of the potential effectiveness of the intervention (Koth, Bradshaw, & Leaf, 2008). This factor can be taken into consideration during the preplanning process before an intervention is introduced or after implementation failure is identified.

Implementation efforts are affected by macrolevel factors that may require broader systems-level change beyond the scope of the immediate implementation feedback system. For instance, implementation quality may show marked variations related to the overall school climate. Research suggests that this global feature plays a role in the structural capacity of the system to support an EBI, whereby higher levels of open communication, support, and orientation to change are associated with higher quality implementation (Kallestad & Olweus, 2003; Parcel et al., 2003). On the other hand, poor staff morale, sense of resignation, and a history of failed intervention attempts have been associated with difficulty implementing and sustaining innovations (Gottfredson & Gottfredson, 2002).

Every community that considers the use of an EBI also has *readiness characteristics*, or characteristics that support or hinder its ability to make change happen. Readiness is considered an important precursor to implementing change. Higher readiness is associated with greater levels of support for change, whereas lower readiness is associated with resistance to change (e.g., Goodman et al., 1998; Macri, Tagliaventi, & Bertolotti, 2002). Recent findings suggest that school functioning, including the school's proactive stance and level of problems, relates to community readiness (Chilenski, Greenberg, & Feinberg, 2007). This work suggests that a sense of empowerment and accomplishment can be built upon in promoting school-based prevention initiatives.

This feedback system can (and should) also occur at a macrolevel. For example, the state of Pennsylvania has rewritten its funding announcements to incorporate quality findings at the local community level. The utilization of EBIs (i.e., Blueprints programs) in the state showed clear connections between various implementation quality measures in the face of local adaptation of EBIs (Bumbarger & Perkins, 2008). As a result, Pennsylvania has rewritten its funding announcements to communities to infuse the creation of a state-level feedback loop regarding the importance of implementation quality of the program for continued funding. This sends a clear message to local community grantees that maintaining implementation quality is essential.

Although preplanning efforts may assist in identifying some macrolevel roadblocks to successful implementation, some initiatives may not be broad enough to overcome such obstacles. However, identifying such concerns at the outset of an initiative enables dialogue between researchers and stakeholders at early stages of the program planning process and helps define expectations.

CONDUCTING PREVENTION RESEARCH IN SCHOOLS

Developing long-term partnerships with a school district may be more unique than common. However, partnering with schools creates excellent opportunities for researchers to consider the scientific process in complex settings and to negotiate designs that maximize outcomes important to both parties. Much of the literature on dissemination thus far illustrates that scaling up with complete fidelity is a myth and that, in actuality, dissemination is a two-way process that changes both the implementation context and the intervention. It is important to note that some changes made by practitioners may actually improve the program's effectiveness. Unfortunately, our understanding of the process of community-driven adaptations is in its early stages. Additional research is necessary to distinguish those adaptations that improve the effectiveness of interventions from those that undermine its impact. Very few of these issues have been studied in depth by prevention scientists and, as such, need to be the focus in the contemporary research agenda.

Contemporary school-based approaches are likely to benefit from the alignment of interest in the utilization of EBIs between researchers and practitioners. As a result of the heightened interest and awareness in producing high-quality outcomes from educational settings, prevention researchers may find themselves in various roles, many of which create contexts for strong potential contributions to existing knowledge. Collaboration is important in all of these situations. This context provides researchers with an opportunity to conduct highly relevant research that informs the process of implementing and disseminating interventions in schools.

As a partner in outcome evaluation, researchers might also engage themselves in implementation research. This might include a focus on descriptive investigations, whereby quantitative or qualitative methods are utilized to study factors affecting program implementation. Dissemination research is still in an exploratory phase, so naturalistic studies of the factors that promote or undermine quality are needed. These types of studies do not require control groups and can often be conducted in the context of service grants.

In addition, research might experimentally vary various parameters of implementation (e.g., dosage, length of training, intensity of coaching). For instance, examinations into the effect of various training methods on the quality of implementation may facilitate use of EBIs by enabling informed and data-driven decisions about context-specific adaptations to implementation methods. Whether descriptively observing the process or systematically investigating the various community-based adaptations, the goal is to understand how to improve our theories in the growing area of implementation science as well as maximize implementation quality.

SUMMARY

The goal of this chapter was to provide a systematic model for collaboratively embarking on research on the implementation of empirically based programs in school settings. We believe that contemporary researchers and practitioners are in a unique position to readily align their priorities and achieve mutually beneficial goals when armed with an awareness of the importance of documentation and monitoring of implementation methods and quality. This process will help intended users to maximize positive outcomes via the realization of a supportive partnership between schools and researchers. Along the way, both parties will benefit from an expanded knowledge base surrounding the complexities of bringing EBIs to scale.

REFERENCES

Allison, K. R., Silverman, G., & Dignam, C. (1990). Effects on students of teacher training in use of a drug education curriculum. *Journal of Drug Education, 20,* 31–46.

Atkins, M. S., Graczyk, P. A., & Frazier, S. L. (2003). Toward a new model for promoting urban children's mental health: Accessible, effective, and sustainable school-based mental health services. *School Psychology Review, 32,* 503–514.

Barrett, S., Bradshaw, C. P., & Lewis-Palmer, T. (2008). Maryland state-wide PBIS initiative: Systems, evaluation, and next steps. *Journal of Positive Behavior Interventions, 10,* 105–114.

Basen-Engquist, K., O'Hara-Tompkins, N., Lovato, C. Y., Lewis, M. J., Parcel, G. S., & Gingiss, P. (1994). The effect of two types of teacher training on implementation of smart choices: A tobacco prevention curriculum. *Journal of School Health, 64,* 334–339.

Battistich, V., Schaps, E., Watson, M., Solomon, D., & Lewis, C. (2000). Effects of the Child Development Project on students' drug use and other problem behaviors. *Journal of Primary Prevention, 21,* 75–99.

Berryhill, J. C., & Prinz, R. J. (2003). Environmental interventions to enhance student adjustment: Implications for prevention. *Prevention Science, 4,* 65–87.

Bumbarger, B. K., & Perkins, D. F. (2008). After randomised trials: Issues related to the dissemination of evidence-based interventions. *Journal of Children's Services, 3*(2), 55–64.

Castro, F. G., Barrera, M., & Martinez, C. R. (2004). The cultural adaptation of preventive interventions: Resolving tensions between fidelity and fit. *Prevention Science, 5,* 41–45.

Catalano, R. F., Berglund, M. L., Ryan, J. A., Lonczak, H. S., & Hawkins, J. D. (2002). Positive youth development in the United States: Research findings on evaluations of positive youth development programs. *Prevention & Treatment, 5,* Article 15. Retrieved August, 1, 2002, from http://journals.apa.org/prevention/volume5/pre0050015a.html

Chen, H. T. (1998). Theory-driven evaluations. *Advances in Educational Productivity, 7,* 15–34.

Chen, H. T. (2003). *Practical program evaluation.* Thousand Oaks, CA: Sage.

Chilenski, S. M., Greenberg, M. T., & Feinberg, M. E. (2007). Community readiness as a multidimensional construct. *Journal of Community Psychology, 35,* 347–368.

Corboy, D., & McDonald, J. (2007). An evaluation of the CAST program using a conceptual model of school-based implementation. *Australian e-Journal for the Advancement of Mental Health, 6*(1). Retrieved March 20, 2008, from http://www.auseinet.com/journal/vol6iss1/corboy.pdf

Dane, A. V., & Schneider, B. H. (1998). Program integrity in primary and secondary prevention: Are implementation effects out of control? *Clinical Psychology Review, 18,* 23–45.

Datnow, A., & Castellano, M. (2000). Teachers' responses to success for all: How beliefs, experiences and expectations shape implementation. *American Educational Research Journal, 37,* 775–799.

Derzon, J. H., Sale, E., Springer, J. F., & Brounstein, P. (2005). Estimating intervention effectiveness: Synthetic projection of field evaluation results. *Journal of Primary Prevention, 26,* 321–343.

Devaney, E., O'Brien, M. U., Resnik, H., Keister, S., & Weissberg, R. P. (2006). *Sustainable schoolwide social and emotional learning: Implementation guide and toolkit.* Chicago: Collaborative for Academic, Social, and Emotional Learning.

Durlak, J. A., & Dupre, E. P. (2008). Implementation matters: A review of research on the influence of implementation on program outcomes and the factors affecting implementation. *American Journal of Community Psychology, 41,* 327–350.

Dusenbury, L., Brannigan, R., & Hansen, W. B. (2005). Quality of implementation: Developing measures crucial to understanding the diffusion of preventive interventions. *Health Education Research, 20,* 308–313.

Dusenbury, L., Hansen, W., Jackson-Newsom, J., Ringwalt, C., Pankratz, M., & Giles, S. (2007, May). *Coaching to implementation quality.* Paper presented at the 15th annual meeting of the Society for Prevention Research, Washington, DC.

Elias, M. J., & Tobias, S. E. (1996). *Social problem solving: Interventions within the schools.* New York: Guilford Press.

Elliott, D. S., & Mihalic, S. (2004). Issues in disseminating and replicating effective prevention programs. *Prevention Science, 5,* 47–52.

Fagan, A. A., & Mihalic S. (2003). Strategies for enhancing the adoption of school-based prevention programs: Lessons learned from the Blueprints for Violence Prevention replications of the Life Skills Training Program. *Journal of Community Psychology, 31,* 235–253.

Fixsen, D. L., Naoom, S. F., Blase, K. F., Friedman, R. M., & Wallace, F. (2005). *Implementation research: A synthesis of the literature* (FMHI Publication No. 231). Tampa: University of South Florida, Louis de la Parte Florida Mental Health Institute, National Implementation Research Network.

Flay, B. R., Biglan, A., Boruch, R. F., Castro, F. G., Gottfredson, D., Kellam, S. G., et al. (2005). *Standards of evidence: Criteria for efficacy, effectiveness and dissemination.* Falls Church, VA: Society for Prevention Research.

Goodman, R. M., Speers, M. A., McLeroy, K., Fawcett, S., Kegler, M., Parker, E., et al. (1998). Identifying and defining the dimensions of community capacity to provide a basis for measurement. *Health Education and Behavior, 25,* 258–278.

Gottfredson, D. C., & Gottfredson, G. D. (2002). Quality of school-based prevention programs: Results from a national survey. *Journal of Research on Crime and Delinquency, 39,* 3–35.

Graczyk, P. A., Domitrovich, C. E., Small, M., & Zins, J. E. (2006). Serving all children: An implementation model framework. *School Psychology Review, 35,* 266–274.

Greenberg, M. T., Domitrovich, C. E., & Bumbarger, B. (2005). The prevention of mental disorders in school-age children: Current state of the field. *Prevention and Treatment, 4,* 1–61.

Greenberg, M. T., Domitrovich, C. E., Graczyk, P. A., & Zins, J. E. (1999). *The study of implementation in school-based preventive interventions: Theory, research, and practice.* Rockville, MD: U.S. Department of Health and Human Services, Substance Abuse and Mental Health Services Administration, Center for Mental Health Services.

Hahn, R., Fuqua-Whitley, D., Wethington, H., Lowy, J., Crosby, A., Fullilove, M., et al. (2007). Effectiveness of universal school-based programs to prevent violent and aggressive behavior: A systematic review. *American Journal of Preventive Medicine, 33*(Suppl. 2), 114–129.

Hallinger, P., & Heck, R. H. (1996). Reassessing the principal's role in school effectiveness: A review of empirical research, 1980–1995. *Educational Administration Quarterly, 32,* 5–44.

Han, S. S., & Weiss, B. (2005). Sustainability of teacher implementation of school-based mental health programs. *Journal of Abnormal Child Psychology, 33,* 665–679.

Joyce, B., & Showers, B. (2002). *Student achievement through staff development* (3rd ed.). Alexandria, VA: Association for Supervision and Curriculum Development.

Kallestad, J. H., & Olweus D. (2003). Predicting teachers' and schools' implementation of the Olweus bullying prevention program: A multilevel study. *Prevention and Treatment, 6*(1), Article 21.

Kam, C., Greenberg, M. T., & Walls, C. T. (2003). Examining the role of implementation quality in school-based prevention using the PATHS curriculum. *Prevention Science, 4,* 55–63.

Kealey, K. A., Peterson, A. V., Jr., Gaul, M. A., & Dinh, K. T. (2000). Teacher training as a behavior change process: Principals and results from a longitudinal study. *Health Education and Behavior, 27,* 64–81.

Kellam, S. G., Koretz, D., & Moscicki, E. K. (1999). Core elements of developmental epidemiologically based prevention research. *American Journal of Community Psychology, 27,* 463–482.

Koth, C. W., Bradshaw, C. P., & Leaf, P. J. (2008). Examining the relationship between classroom-level factors and students' perception of school climate. *Journal of Educational Psychology, 100,* 96–104.

Macri, D. M., Tagliaventi, M. R., & Bertolotti, F. (2002). A grounded theory for resistance to change in a small organization. *Journal of Organizational Change Management, 15,* 292–310.

McCormick, L. K., Steckler, A. B., & McLeroy, K. R. (1995). Diffusion of innovations in schools: A study of adoption and implementation of school-based tobacco prevention curricula. *American Journal of Health Promotion, 9,* 210–219.

McNeal, R. B., Hansen, W. B., Harrington, N. G., & Giles, S. M. (2004). How All Stars works: An examination of program effects on mediating variables. *Health Education and Behavior, 31,* 165–178.

Mihalic, S., Irwin, K., Fagan, A., Ballard, D., & Elliott, D. (2004, July). Successful program implementation: Lessons from blueprints. *Juvenile Justice Bulletin.* Washington, DC: U.S. Department of Justice, Office of Justice Programs. Retrieved February 18, 2008, from http://www.ncjrs.gov/pdffiles1/ojjdp/204273.pdf

Moncher, F. J., & Prinz, R. J. (1991). Treatment fidelity in outcome studies. *Clinical Psychology Review, 11,* 247–266.

Mrazek, P. J., & Haggerty, R. J. (1994). *Reducing risks for mental disorders: Frontiers for preventive intervention research.* Washington, DC: National Academies Press, National Academy of Sciences, Institute of Medicine, Division of Biobehavioral Sciences and Mental Disorders, Committee on Prevention of Mental Disorders.

Noell, G. H., Witt, J. C., Slider, N. J., Connell, J. E., Gatti, S. L., Williams, K. L., et al. (2005). Treatment implementation following behavioral consultation in schools: A comparison of three follow-up strategies. *School Psychology Review, 34,* 87–106.

Parcel, G. S., Perry, C. L., Kelder, S. H., Elder, J. P., Mitchell, P. D., Lytle, L. A., et al. (2003). School climate and the institutionalization of the CATCH program. *Health Education and Behavior, 30,* 489–502.

Patton, M. Q. (1979). Evaluation of program implementation. *Evaluation Studies Review Annual, 4,* 318–345.

Payne A. A., Gottfredson D. C., & Gottfredson G. D. (2006). School predictors of the intensity of implementation of school-based prevention programs. *Prevention Science, 7,* 225–237.

Penuel, W. R., Fishman, B. J., Yamaguchi, R., & Gallagher, L. P. (2007). What makes professional development effective? Strategies that foster curriculum implementation. *American Educational Research Journal, 44,* 921–958.

Perry, C. L., Murray, D. M., & Griffin, G. (1990). Evaluating the statewide dissemination of smoking prevention curricula: Factors in teacher compliance. *Journal of School Health, 60,* 501–504.

Putnam, R. T., & Borko, H. (2000). What do new views of knowledge and thinking have to say about research on teacher learning? *Educational Researcher, 29,* 4–15.

Ramey, C. T., Ramey, S. L., & Lanzi, R. G. (2006). Children's health and education. In K. A. Renninger, I. E. Sigel, W. Damon, & R. M. Lerner (Eds.), *Handbook of child psychology: Vol. 4. Child psychology in practice* (6th ed., pp. 864–892). Hoboken, NJ: Wiley.

Ringwalt, C. L., Ennett, S., Johnson, R., Rohrbach, L. A., Simons-Rudolph, A., Vincus, A., & Thorne, J. (2003). Factors associated with fidelity to substance use prevention curriculum guides in the nation's middle schools. *Health Education and Behavior, 30,* 375–391.

Rogers, E. M. (2003). *Diffusion of innovations* (2nd ed.). New York: Free Press.

Rohrbach, L. A., Grana, R., Sussman, S., & Valente, T. W. (2006). Type II translation: Transporting prevention interventions from research to real-world settings. *Evaluation and the Health Profession, 29,* 302–333.

Rohrbach, L. A., Graham, J. W., & Hansen, W. B. (1993). Diffusion of a school-based substance abuse prevention program: Predictors of program implementation. *Preventive Medicine, 22,* 237–260.

Rohrbach, L. A., Ringwalt, C. L., Ennett, S. T., & Vincus, A. A. (2005). Factors associated with adoption of evidence-based substance use prevention curricula in U.S. school districts. *Health Education Research, 20,* 514–526.

Romanz, T. E., Kantor, J. H., & Elias, M. (2003). Implementation and evaluation of urban school-wide social–emotional learning programs. *Evaluation and Program Planning, 27,* 89–103.

Rose, D. J., & Church, R. J. (1998). Learning to teach: The acquisition and maintenance of teaching skills. *Journal of Behavioral Education, 8,* 5–35.

Skara, S., Rohrbach, L. A., Sun, P., & Sussman, S. (2005). An evaluation of the fidelity of implementation of a school-based drug abuse prevention program: Project Toward No Drug Abuse (TND). *Journal of Drug Education, 35,* 305–329.

Tobler, N. S., Roona, M. R., Ochshorn, P., Marshall, D. G., Streke, A. V., & Stackpole, K. M. (2000). School-based adolescent drug prevention programs: 1998 meta-analysis. *Journal of Primary Prevention, 20,* 275–337.

Wandersman, A. (2003). Community science: Bridging the gap between science and practice with community-centered models. *American Journal of Community Psychology, 31,* 227–241.

Weissberg, R. P., & Greenberg, M. T. (1998). Prevention science and community collaborative action research: Combining the best from both perspectives. *Journal of Mental Health, 7,* 477–490.

Wilson, D. B., Gottfredson, D. C., & Najaka, S. S. (2001). School-based prevention of problem behaviors: A meta-analysis. *Journal of Quantitative Criminology, 17,* 247–272.

Woolf, S. H. (2008). The meaning of translational research and why it matters. *Journal of the American Medical Association, 299,* 211–213.

7

In Vivo Testing of Learning and Instructional Principles: The Design and Implementation of School-Based Experimentation

Gwen A. Frishkoff, Gregory White, and Charles A. Perfetti

This chapter is intended for researchers who are interested in conducting studies within school settings using experimental designs. The goal for such studies is to test ideas about the causes of, and contexts for, learning in the classroom. This work may be critical for connecting lab-based research on learning and cognition to studies of learning in real-world settings. For this reason, school-based experimentation has the potential to yield results with strong practical, as well as basic scientific, relevance.

We begin this chapter with a discussion of several issues that can inform the design of school-based research. We then consider three categories of experimental research—(a) lab-based experiments, (b) school-based interventions (efficacy and effectiveness studies), and (c) an emergent category of research known as school-based (or in vivo) experimentation—and discuss their pros and cons. Next, we present some examples of school-based experimentation and consider the use of computational tools and technologies to enable this kind of research. Beyond the translation of research into practice, school-based experimentation can support classroom research that feeds back to refine theories of learning. It can therefore serve not only as a testbed for small-scale studies of efficacy ("what works") but also as a research platform for scientific discovery (Walker, Koedinger, McLaren, & Rummel, 2006). In this way, in vivo experimentation may come to be viewed as a "bridging methodology," which can help to link theories and models of learning to actual improvements in school-based learning and instruction.

UNDERSTANDING "WHAT WORKS"—AND WHY

Given the recent focus on high-stakes testing in schools, stakeholders in education—parents, teachers, and policymakers—are increasingly looking to published research for guidelines on "what works" to boost classroom achievement (Lagemann, 2000; Levin, 2004; Mayer, 2003; Shavelson & Towne, 2002; Town, Wise, & Winters, 2005; Whitehurst, 2003; see also http://ies.ed.gov/ncee/wwc/). In line with this interest, federal funding priorities have shifted to support research with clear practical as well as scientific import (Whitehurst, 2003). With these shifts in funding policies, researchers are recognizing new opportunities for collaborative research with schools that can advance the science of learning and instruction. To improve their chances for success, researchers would be well advised to consider the unique challenges of conducting experimental research within schools.

In this section, we discuss three specific issues that can inform the design of school-based research: (a) the grain size of the research question, (b) the relative emphasis on basic and applied goals, and (c) consideration of internal and external validity of research outcomes. We then describe four categories of research on learning and instruction, including three experimental research paradigms, and discuss their merits with respect to these three issues.

Grain Size of the Research Question

In defining the goals for a particular study, an important consideration is the grain size of the research question (Anderson & Gluck, 2001). Is the goal to investigate learning at a neurocognitive level, as it unfolds over tens or hundreds of milliseconds? Or is the goal to observe learning that lasts over hours and days? These goals are different, though not mutually exclusive. A single study can use multiple measures to link changes in (neuro-)cognitive processes to outcomes on written tests that are administered hours or days later (e.g., Ansari & Coch, 2005; Frishkoff, Collins-Thompson,

Perfetti, & Callan, 2008; Frishkoff, Perfetti, & Collins-Thompson, 2009; McClelland, Fiez, & McCandliss, 2002). For practical reasons, however, most studies focus on one or two measures that target a particular level of analysis.

Questions that target learning at a finer grained level will generally require more frequent sampling of behavior and different research methods than studies of learning at a larger grain size. For example, there is a long history of research on vocabulary learning and retention over hours, days, or weeks (see Beck, McKeown, & Kucan, 2002, for a review). To measure these effects, researchers have used standardized assessments of vocabulary skills, together with oral and written tests of word knowledge administered before and after instruction. These tests are practical and often highly efficient because they are inexpensive, standardized, and can often be group administered.

More recently, researchers have used methods such as event-related brain potentials (Frishkoff, Perfetti, & Collins-Thompson, 2009; Frishkoff, Perfetti, & Westbury, 2009; Mestres-Misse, Rodriguez-Fornells, & Munte, 2007; Perfetti, Wloko, & Hart, 2005) and eye tracking (Reichle, Rayner, & Pollatskek, 2003) to investigate word-learning processes that take place within tens and hundreds of milliseconds—the timescale at which cognition actually unfolds during learning (Anderson & Gluck, 2001). These studies provide windows into the component processes that take place in the learner's mind as she processes new words during meaning acquisition. Researchers can therefore use these methods to address questions about how different contexts affect moment-by-moment changes in specific perceptual, cognitive, and motivational processes in the learner. For example, Frishkoff, Perfetti, and Collins-Thompson (2009) observed different patterns of brain activity associated with word learning that is more or less robust, as indicated by later performance on posttest assessments of word knowledge. These neural dynamics may in turn be linked to different aspects of word semantic learning, such as active retrieval of words from memory versus "automatic" priming that reflects more robust knowledge. In this way, cognitive science methods provide a way to link detailed models of learning and cognition to outcomes that actually matter for students and teachers.

FRISHKOFF, WHITE, AND PERFETTI

Given the technology that is needed to track learning at the subsecond scale, it might seem that fine-grained measures of learning would be feasible only in the lab. In fact, new instructional technologies are enabling research designs that would not have been possible 5 or 10 years ago. For example, two well-known programs for computer-supported learning of reading, math, and science now support measurement of student behavior during learning over tens of milliseconds (Anderson, Corbett, Koedinger, & Pelletier, 2005). As analysis and interpretation of these data become more sophisticated, they are revealing insights into cognitive dynamics during complex tasks, which can be carried out in a classroom context (typically, at computer workstations) as well as in the laboratory. For example, Anderson and Gluck (2001) described the use of eye tracking alongside their widely used Algebra Tutor. When interacting with complex visual displays, people commonly shift their gaze to examine different parts of the scene. The question addressed by Anderson and Gluck was whether these visual shifts of attention could be used to detect when students were attending to irrelevant information or when they had skipped essential information that was needed to provide correct input to the tutor. By supporting these kinds of inferences, eye tracking allows the tutor to respond to student errors with appropriate feedback and support.

Basic, Applied, and Translational Research Goals

The distinction between fine-grained measures of learning (moment-by-moment changes in neurocognition) and—at the other extreme— large-scale interventions can be related to the contrast between basic and applied research (Flay, 1986; Rychetnik, Frommier, Hawe, & Shiell, 2002). Basic research (science for the sake of discovery) and applied research (science for the solution to practical problems) can, in turn, be roughly aligned with two categories of educational research as characterized (most recently) by the Institute of Educational Sciences (IES) request for proposals (http://ies.ed.gov). The IES was established by the U.S. Department of Education in 2003, with the explicit charge of advancing evidence-based research in education. The IES framework for federally funded research articulates a set of principles and categories that are grounded in a long history of scientific research (Towne, Wise, & Winters, 2005). It is therefore of scientific, as well as pragmatic, importance for researchers to be familiar with this framework.

Research that is focused on development and testing of learning principles fits with IES's current Goal 2 ("development") research and is congruent with what Levin & O'Donnell have termed "Stage 2" of an evidence-based program of educational research (Levin, O'Donnell, & Kratochwill, 2003). The motivation for development studies is to investigate underlying causes or mechanisms of learning: *Why* is a particular intervention hypothesized to yield better student outcomes, relative to current education practices (http://ies.ed.gov)? The emphasis on causal mechanisms of learning and instruction is congruent with the traditional goals of basic research, where the primary interest is to design and test *principles* of learning and instruction. For example: Does spaced versus massed practice leads to improved learning? When is feedback helpful during student learning? "Why"-focused studies are integral to the development and testing of theories, which may in turn inform the strategic design of instructional methods and school-based interventions.

In the "what works" phase, the goal is to study practical outcomes—that is, student learning—that can be causally linked to an instructional intervention. The intervention is typically defined at a fairly coarse-grained level (i.e., measures of learning over days, weeks, and months). In traditional terms, what-works studies could be classified as applied research. Studies that address questions at this level fit with IES Goal 3 (*efficacy*) or Goal 4 (*effectiveness*), depending on their scale of implementation (http://ies.ed.gov; see also Flay, 1986), and align with "Stage 2" and "Stage 3," respectively, within the framework of Levin and O'Donnell (Levin, O'Donnell, & Kratochwill, 2003). The motivation for efficacy research (Goal 2) is to identify contexts under which an intervention yields statistically significant and practically relevant educational outcomes (http://ies.ed.gov). Effectiveness studies (Goal 3) take this goal one step further, by aiming to determine whether a particular intervention works at a larger scale and across a variety of contexts. In both efficacy and effectiveness research, the goal is to determine what instructional practices lead to meaningful gains in student learning (where "meaningful" implies medium-to-large effect sizes; cf. chap. 6).

It is tempting simply to equate why and what-works studies with the traditional categories of basic and applied research, but this is not quite accurate. Questions about learning and instructional principles ("why" questions) are often motivated by the desire to understand and improve classroom learning. This is not science "for science's sake," autonomous from practical interests and goals, but is better classified as *translational research*, that is, research that is motivated by an interest in practical applications but is formulated in a way that can lead to new scientific discoveries. Research that fits this description has also been called "oriented basic research" (Stokes, 1997, p. 66) and "use-inspired basic research" (Stokes, 1997, p. 73, Figure 3.5). School-based research on learning and instruction may be naturally aligned with this bridging category: Within a translational research agenda, "why" questions may be formulated with an eye to real-world challenges of supporting robust learning in the classroom (Exhibit 7.1).

Internal and External Validity of Results

Once the goals have been articulated for a particular study—which includes consideration of grain size of the research question and practical significance (e.g., relevance for classroom learning)—it is imperative to consider how to achieve these goals in a way that leads to high-quality research results. In scientific research, high-quality studies are characterized by methods that are empirically based, are statistically reliable, and allow for independent replication (Shavelson & Towne, 2002; Towne et al., 2005). High-quality *experimental* research is further characterized by *internal validity*, which requires proof of a relationship between an experimental manipulation (independent variable) and measures of learning (dependent variable).

The goal of practical relevance, or *external validity*, is another matter, but one that is equally important to achieving high-quality outcomes for school-based research. A learning study may meet the most rigorous criteria for scientific validity and may yield statistically significant results. However, the test of practical relevance is whether these results can be expected to generalize beyond the experiment context, that is, whether

Exhibit 7.1

"Instrumentation of Learning" in Schools

 Ken Koedinger is a professor in the computer science and psychology departments at Carnegie Mellon University. He is also codirector of the Pittsburgh Science of Learning Center (PSLC). Koedinger's research has contributed new principles and techniques for the design of educational software and has produced basic cognitive science research results on the nature of mathematical thinking and learning.

Gwen Frishkoff (GF): The PSLC states that its primary mission is "pave the way to an understanding of robust learning" (http://www. learnlab.org). What is "robust learning," and how does it differ from the kind of learning that we are used to seeing in the laboratory?

Ken Koedinger (KK): So the phrase "robust learning" I started using [in] recognition of the education wars. It seemed like we needed to find a way to get beyond the debates [about] whether conceptual understanding was what we were after, or procedural fluency—toward the sense that both are important, particularly when we want students' learning to be robust, meaning (1) *to last well after the instruction*—so robust over time; (2) to be able *to apply in new situations,* in traditional terms, transfer; and (3) *setting a foundation to help students more efficiently learn other things.*

GF: What are some methods that PSLC researchers use to study robust learning in schools?

KK: Well, there's this idea of *in vivo experimentation.* And it's not totally new, but it is different from at least three things. It's different

(continued)

Exhibit 7.1

"Instrumentation of Learning" in Schools (*Continued*)

from *lab studies,* which have strong internal validity, but not such great external validity. It's different from *design research,* which is in the classroom, but doesn't have a control group, except perhaps in rare situations. It's very much driven through a collaboration with practice—and is Stokes-like in character—but it's all about the ecological validity, and it's about case-based qualitative research. And the third one is a *randomized field trial.* The standard randomized field trial has internal and external validity. It's in the classroom, and it's also controlled. But the standard randomized field trial is not a scientific study. It's a policy study. It's about whether this program—like Cognitive Tutor Algebra—is better. It's a "What Works" study. It's not about [testing] a scientific principle, and why does this particular principle work. Now, we do randomize assignment in in vivo experimentation, but what differentiates it from these grand randomized field trials is that we're focused on an individual principle that's one variable away from the control condition. Therefore, it's principle testing, it's in the classroom, and it's got control.

GF: Can you give an example and explain how it has led to new insights into robust learning?

KK: Well, one of our early studies was looking at whether we could get self-explanation to work in a computer-based tutoring system. Doing the study with the technology and in the classroom allowed a number of things. For one thing, we showed that we could implement self-explanation in a way that could be quite cost-effectively delivered, because it's implemented in the technology in a tutor that's now being used by hundreds of thousands of students across the country. In that study, students provided explanations by citing glossary entries. So it wasn't the full self-explanation that's implemented in some of the lab studies, but that menu-based thing

Exhibit 7.1

"Instrumentation of Learning" in Schools (*Continued*)

worked. We also had a number of different measures to get at robust learning and transfer, as well as log data. And one of the interesting things scientifically that that revealed is that—you know, this is part of the argument for robust learning—if you just looked at straightforward problem solving, there was no difference between the two conditions (between the self-explanation condition and [the condition in which] students were just practicing with the tutor without self-explanation). We controlled for time, which is an important thing, meaning the self-explainers did about half as many problems as the problem-solving group. So the problem-solving group was getting more practice. If we looked at their learning curves at the end of the tutor, they were actually doing a little bit better at their problem-solving skills compared with the self-explanation [group]. But even the simple view of the move from the tutor to the test was that the more robust learning acquired by the explanation group allowed them to catch up on the problem-solving items on the test. And then on the harder items, where we said "You may or may not have enough information to solve this problem," the problem-solving group (in a rather nonreflective way) will just bull ahead and give an answer as if it's justified, you know, reflecting a lack of conceptual understanding and maybe even a lack of metacognitive control—to say "Wait a minute, hold it. Do I really know this is true?" Corresponding with this, we actually saw a higher ratio of omission errors (in the self-explanation group). They're more likely to say, "I don't know," [whereas] the [control] group is more likely to jump in.

GF: Along those same lines, can you give some examples of how this approach can be used to study metacognitive and affective processes in learning?

(*continued*)

Exhibit 7.1

"Instrumentation of Learning" in Schools (*Continued*)

KK: [One example is the work] Rich Mayer has done looking at personalization and politeness and their role in learning. And we had taken one of his principles and tried to apply it in a chemistry course. And this is one of those examples where just because it has worked in the lab doesn't mean it's going to work in vivo. The personalization effort in the Stochiometry Tutor did not lead to improved learning—at least as it was implemented. Part of the mystery that is still ongoing is why. We're trying to do more data collection now. We've instrumented the tutors to collect learning data throughout the semester. If we could also instrument them to occasionally ask survey questions about motivation, then we could get at these issues over time.

GF: What do you mean by "instrumenting of tutors"?

KK: I heard this interesting story recently [which illustrates the notion of "instrumentation" and how it can lead to new data and new insights]. We all know about FedEx and about how great a success it is. It was pitched to like five investor groups, and they were all like, "Why would you want to put labels on packages?" Because that was the pitch: that they all get time-stamped. They'd have labels where they came from, where they ended up. They put all of this in a database, and then they were going to run optimization algorithms to figure out how to make things efficient enough to do it overnight. So, we always think of FedEx—"Oh, they had the idea for overnight shipping." Well, really, the real idea was [to] collect the data first. Educational technology is the instrumentation of courses—of online courses, of blended courses—in a way that I think is going to have a similar kind of revolutionary impact on education.

they translate to real-world settings (i.e., classrooms). For learning research to have practical relevance for education, it must have high external as well as high internal validity.

Unfortunately, it is difficult to ensure high internal and high external validity in a single study. In fact, it is informative to contrast different research designs along these two dimensions (Figure 7.1), because this makes clear the trade-offs that are inherent to traditional research designs. Lab-based experimentation (Category 1, Figure 7.1) is generally characterized by high internal, but low external, validity. Laboratory designs allow for rigorous control of the independent variables, which tends to strengthen the comparison of the experimental (treatment) versus control conditions. The trade-off is that, precisely by limiting the context for the experiment manipulations, lab experiments may produce statistically significant effects that do not generalize to real-world settings. Statistical significance does

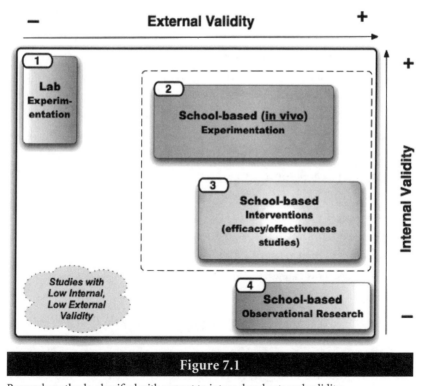

Figure 7.1

Research methods, classified with respect to internal and external validity.

FRISHKOFF, WHITE, AND PERFETTI

not necessarily translate to practical significance. What is clearly an advantage in terms of statistical control is a potential disadvantage when the goal is to establish results that generalize to a wide range of contexts.

By the same token, research results that hold up in school settings (Category 3, Figure 7.1) have perforce met the criterion of external validity, despite the characteristic lack of control over many aspects of instructional delivery and conditions for measurement of student learning. For example, while efficacy and effectiveness studies are designed to address practical questions about the outcomes of school-based interventions, they are generally more limited in their ability to address questions about the underlying mechanisms that lead to optimal learning and instruction.

A third category of research involves *nonexperimental* (e.g., qualitative) methods, including observational and design studies (Category 4, Figure 7.1). These methods can provide very rich sources of evidence on learning and instruction. In addition, school-based observational research tends to have high external validity, to the extent that observations are carried out in authentic classroom settings, with minimal interference by the researcher. By the same token, however, nonexperimental studies cannot support causal inferences (Raudenbush, 2005) and are therefore unable to address either why or what-works questions about learning and instruction. They may be most useful and appropriate during the hypothesis formation and design stages of a research program.

Finally, a fourth type of research has recently emerged: school-based experimental research, or *in vivo experimentation* (Category 3, Figure 7.1) an approach that has been pioneered by researchers within the Pittsburgh Science of Learning Center as described in Exhibit 7.1. Here the goal is to design studies that have high internal validity—are rigorous and controlled—and high external validity—because they are conducted within school settings. This category of research is the focus of the next section.

IN VIVO EXPERIMENTATION

Experimental research has provided key evidence on the nature of human learning (Anderson, Corbett, Koedinger, & Pelletier, 1995; Anderson & Gluck, 2001; Bransford, Brown, & Cocking, 2000; Glaser, 1987, 2001; Klahr,

Chen, & Toth, 2001; White, Frishkoff, & Bullock, 2008). However, efforts to translate laboratory findings into meaningful student outcomes have yielded mixed results (Raudenbush, 2005). Researchers and educators alike now know better than to expect a seamless transition from laboratory science to classroom practice.

Advances in learning technologies are providing new opportunities for bridging the gap between the laboratory and the classroom. One example of this forward thinking is the adoption of computer systems, such as intelligent tutors, for use in the classroom. In addition to providing support for classroom learning, these methods are enabling new designs for translational research—that is, studies that are scientifically grounded and are linked to interventions with proven effectiveness in schools. Next, we provide a brief introduction to computer-based learning and instructional tools and technologies. We then discuss several cases that illustrate how technology can support school-based research that is both rigorous and practically significant.

Computer-Aided Learning and Instruction

Computer-aided instruction is not new. In the 1960s, Richard Atkinson and colleagues developed a computer system to support early reading and applied this technology in a series of word-learning experiments (Atkinson, 1972), using experiment designs that are remarkably similar to recent studies of computer-aided vocabulary instruction (e.g., Marsh, Roediger, Bjork, & Bjork, 2007; Pavlik & Anderson, 2005). More generally, computer-aided instruction has been a mainstay of research in artificial intelligence and the cognitive sciences since the 1960s, and has led to a variety of school-based applications of learning and instructional technologies in the last 5 decades (Bransford et al., 2005). As discussed below, there have been some impressive efforts to translate cognitive theories of learning and cognition into tangible tools that can be used for research as well as direct educational applications.

Educational research has benefited from the use of a particular kind of computer-aided instruction, known as *intelligent tutoring systems* (ITS). ITS are computer systems that display problems or questions for students to answer and provide feedback on performance in the form of hints, attentional cues, definitions, equations, or other information that is intended to support improved performance (Van Lehn, 2006; Van Lehn, Koedinger, et al., 2007). Intelligent tutoring systems have been developed to support student learning in a variety of content areas, including vocabulary (Pavlik & Anderson, 2005), reading comprehension (Graesser et al., 2004), mathematics (Ritter, Anderson, Koedinger, & Corbett, 2007), and science (Van Lehn et al., 2007). More recently, intelligent tutors have been designed to support metacognitive, as well as domain-specific, learning (Cen, Koedinger, & Junker, 2006; Graesser, McNamara, & Van Lehn, 2005).

ITS that make use of cognitive models are referred to as *cognitive tutors* (Anderson & Gluck, 2001; Walker et al., 2006). Models of human cognition can be used to refine computer-aided support for student learning: When learner performance deviates from the correct (target) model, the system can provide additional problems or feedback to steer the learner back on course. Figure 7.2 illustrates how such models can be applied to support efficient and effective learning of vocabulary. By comparing student performance with the idealized (cognitive) model, cognitive tutors can estimate student learning at a fine-grained cognitive level, leading to more detailed—and potentially more accurate—feedback and assessment (Cen et al., 2006).

The use of technology is not a magic bullet; indeed, computer-based instruction can introduce its own challenges and trade-offs: for example, if the software interface is not intuitive, there can be a learning curve associated with the use of the technology itself (Van Lehn et al., 2005). However, the range of applications for tutoring systems, as well as their proven efficacy in some domains, suggests that they are likely to play an important role in school-based learning for years to come. Furthermore, these technologies can afford some unique opportunities for school-based research and can help to address some of the methodological issues raised earlier in the chapter.

Tools for Embedded Assessment

Translational research, as discussed earlier, seeks to engineer studies with both high internal and high external validity. Cognitive tutors can support

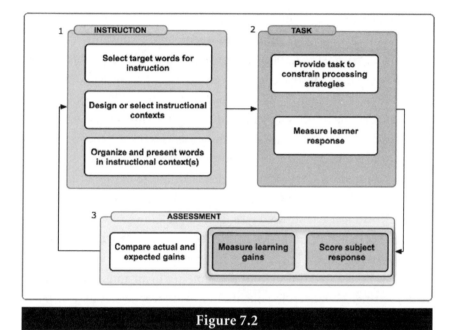

Figure 7.2

Design for adaptive vocabulary instruction. (1) Instructional design components include methods for selection of target words and methods for selection and presentation of instructional materials. (2) Task includes instructions provided to learner and measurement of learner response on each learning trial. (3) Assessment provides information on the success or failure of learning at each step.

both these goals by allowing for manipulation of a single instructional component (Walker et al., 2006). In addition, researchers at the Pittsburgh Science of Learning Center (PSLC) have developed tools to support what Koedinger has termed *instrumentation of learning* (see Exhibit 7.1), that is, measurement of learning at a fine-grained level in the classroom. PSLC studies are often carried out within LearnLab courses (http://www.learn lab.org), in which students complete homework and some in-class exercises using ITS that record their behavior in great detail. These data are subsequently analyzed by using analysis software that allows researchers to test hypotheses about the *knowledge components* that make up a complex task (Cen, Keodinger, & Junker, 2006; Koedinger & Alevan, 2007; Van Lehn et al., 2007). The notion of a "knowledge component" captures the idea that mastery of a particular topic (e.g., computing the area of a circle) may require students to become proficient with several component processes ("processes" is deliberately vague here—concepts, skills, and steps are all possible examples of knowledge components on this model). Researchers aim to construct detailed models of the knowledge components in a particular domain. They can then work with teachers and domain experts to develop tutoring systems that are designed to support learner mastery of each component. If the researcher's model is correct, then mastery of these components should lead to learning that is truly robust. Often, this requires continuous assessment of student learning, so the tutor (or teacher) can infer which component skills or concepts a student seems to be lacking.

As Koedinger has stressed (see Exhibit 7.1), in vivo experimentation is unique in that it supports well controlled experiments, which can be carried out in real classroom settings. In principle, student knowledge of a topic can be assessed throughout the semester in an authentic ("embedded") setting. Moreover, in collaboration with teachers, it may be possible to test whether learning that took place with a cognitive tutor translates into student gains on other tasks (e.g., teacher-assigned homework, in-class exams).

Tools for Individualized Instruction

The use of computer-aided instruction (and of cognitive tutors in particular) has an additional benefit, namely, that it can support instruction that is individualized and adaptive. In this context, *adaptive* refers to the ability to shape instructional events in response to learner performance, which gives clues about the specific concepts or skills that the learner needs to practice at a given point in time. The automated nature of computer-based instruction allows it to be effective, in principle, by providing instructional materials that are selected to optimize learning, by specifying constraints on selection and presentation of instructional contexts. For example, if the tutor detects that a learner is confused about the connotation (positive or negative emotional valence) of a word, then on subsequent learning trials the tutor can provide feedback to the learner to highlight this particular feature of the word (Brown, Frishkoff, & Eskenazi, 2005; Frishkoff, Collins-Thompson, et al., 2008).

In addition to these practical implications, continuous measurement of learner behavior can lead to new research insights, providing important constraints on theories and models of student learning. For example, Frishkoff and associates (Frishkoff, Collins-Thompson, et al., 2008) recently developed a method for automatic scoring of free-response data in a meaning-generation task. This method allows for measurement of gradual changes in word knowledge and is sensitive to a variety of manipulations, including individual differences in reading and vocabulary skills, spaced versus massed learning of words in context, and variations in contextual support for word learning. We envision that this method could be modified and extended to support an adaptive, computer-based framework for vocabulary training, along the lines of what is shown in Figure 7.2.

In principle, adaptive protocols should lead to more efficient learning than instructional designs that present the same words in the same contexts for each learner. Individuals know different words and have different cognitive and language skills when they begin instruction. Moreover, the precise trajectory of learning for a given individual is hard to predict, because it is likely to depend on a number of (as yet unknown) factors. Therefore, an instructional protocol that can be modified online, in response to learner performance, may be more likely to result in optimal learning.

SUMMARY

We began the chapter by discussing the trade-off between scientific rigor and practical relevance in the design of school-based experiments. We then described new research tools and technologies that can be used to address this trade-off. Computer-based tutoring systems can implement basic learning principles and have evolved to the point where they are routinely used in classrooms to support student learning. In addition, these systems can be used to design and implement school-based studies that test learning hypotheses at a fine-grained, cognitive level. Computer-based instructional systems allow for a moderate degree of control over measurement and implementation. At the same time, they may have strong relevance for school-based learning and instruction, precisely because they can be embedded in practice, which allows for fine-grained "instrumentation of learning" (Exhihibt 7.1) over weeks and even months. In this way, new research tools may come to be viewed as bridging technologies, which can connect observations of learning at a very fine grain size to practical outcomes that matter for real-world learning and instruction. This is precisely the type of research that can help bridge the gap from experimental results on learning to rigorous and relevant school-based research.

REFERENCES

Anderson, J. R., Corbett, A. T., Koedinger, K., & Pelletier, R. (1995). Cognitive tutors: Lessons learned. *Journal of Learning Sciences, 4,* 167–207.

Anderson, J. R., & Gluck, K. A. (2001). What role do cognitive architectures play in intelligent tutoring systems? In S. M. Carver & D. Klahr (Eds.), *Cognition and instruction: Twenty five years of progress* (pp. 227–261). Mahwah, NJ: Erlbaum.

Ansari, D., & Coch, D. (2006). Bridges over troubled waters: Education and cognitive neuroscience. *Trends in Cognitive Science, 10*(4), 146–151.

Atkinson, R. C. (1972). Ingredients for a theory of instruction. *American Psychologist, 27,* 921–931.

Beck, I., McKeown, M., & Kucan, L. (2002). *Bringing words to life: Robust vocabulary instruction.* New York: Guilford Press.

Bransford, J. D., Brown, A. L., & Cocking, R. R. (Eds.). (2000). *How people learn: Brain, mind, experience, and school.* Washington, DC: National Academies Press.

Brown, J., Frishkoff, G. A., & Eskenazi, M. (2005). Automatic question generation for vocabulary assessment. In *Proceedings of the Conference on Human Language Technology* (pp. 819–826). Morristown, NJ: Association for Computational Linguistics.

Cen, H., Koedinger, K., & Junker, B. (2006, June 26–30). Learning Factors Analysis— A General Method for Cognitive Model Evaluation and Improvement. Paper presented at *The 8th International Conference on Intelligent Tutoring Systems,* Jhongli, Taiwan.

Flay, B. R. (1986). Efficacy and effectiveness trials (and other phases of research) in the development of health promotion programs. *Preventative Medicine, 15,* 451–474.

Frishkoff, G., Collins-Thompson, K., Perfetti, C., & Callan, J. (2008). Measuring incremental changes in word knowledge: Experimental validation and implications for learning and assessment. *Behavioral Research Methods, 40,* 907–925.

Frishkoff, G. A., Perfetti, C. A., & Collins-Thompson, K. (2009, in press). Lexical quality in the brain: ERP evidence for robust word learning from context. *Developmental Neuropsychology.*

Frishkoff, G. A., Perfetti, C. A., & Westbury, C. (2009). ERP measures of partial semantic knowledge: Left temporal indices of skill differences and lexical quality. *Biological Psychology, 80*(1), 130–147.

Glaser, R. (1987). Learning theories and theories of knowledge. In E. DeCorte, J. G. L. C. Lodewijks, R. Parmentier, & P. Span (Eds.), *Learning and instruction* (pp. 397–414). Oxford, England/Leuven, Belgium: Pergamon Press/Leuven University Press.

Glaser, R. (2001). Progress then and now. In S. M. Carver & D. Klahr (Eds.), *Cognition and instruction: Twenty five years of progress* (pp. 493–508). Mahwah, NJ: Erlbaum.

Graesser, A. C., Lu, S., Jackson, G. T., Mitchell, H. H., Ventura, M., Olney, A., et al. (2004). Autotutor: A tutor with dialogue in natural language. *Behavioral Research Methods, Instruments, and Computers, 36,* 180–192.

Graesser, A. C., McNamara, D. S., & Van Lehn, K. (2005). Scaffolding Deep Comprehension Strategies through Point&Query, AutoTutor, and iSTART. *Educational Psychologist, 40*(4), 225–234.

Klahr, D., Chen, Z., & Toth, E. E. (2001). Cognitive development and science education: Ships passing in the night or beacons of mutual illumination? In S. M. Carver & D. Klahr (Eds.), *Cognition and instruction: Twenty five years of progress* (pp. 75–120). Mahwah, NJ: Erlbaum.

Koedinger, K., & Alevan, V. (2007). Exploring the assistance dilemma in experiments with cognitive tutors. *Educational Psychology Review, 19,* 239–264.

Lagemann, E. C. (2000). *An elusive science: The troubling history of education research.* Chicago: University of Chicago.

Levin, J. R. (2004). Random thoughts on the (in)credibility of educational-psychological intervention research. *Educational Psychologist, 39*(3), 174–184.

Levin, J. R., O'Donnell, A. M., & Kratochwill, T. R. (2003). Educational/psychological intervention research. In W. Reynolds & C. Miller (Eds.), *Handbook of Psychology, Vol. 7: Educational Psychology* (pp. 557–581). Hoboken, NJ: John Wiley & Sons.

Marsh, E. J., Roediger, H. L., III, Bjork, R. A., & Bjork, E. L. (2007). The memorial consequences of multiple-choice testing. *Psychonomic Bulletin Review, 14,* 194–199.

Mayer, R. E. (2003). Learning environments: The case for evidence-based practice and issue-driven research. *Educational Psychology Review, 15,* 359–366.

McClelland, J. L., Fiez, J. A., & McCandliss, B. D. (2002). Teaching the /r/–/l/ discrimination to Japanese adults: Behavioral and neural aspects. *Physiology and Behavior, 77,* 657–662.

Mestres-Misse, A., Rodriguez-Fornells, A., & Munte, T. F. (2007). Watching the brain during meaning acquisition. *Cerebral Cortex, 17,* 1858–1866.

Pavlik, P., & Anderson, J. R. (2005). Practice and forgetting effects on vocabulary memory: An activation-based model of the spacing effect. *Cognitive Science, 29,* 559–586.

Perfetti, C. A., Wlotko, E. W., & Hart, L. A. (2005). Word learning and individual differences in word learning reflected in event-related potentials. *Journal of Experimental Psychology: Learning, Memory, & Cognition, 31*(6), 1281–1292.

Raudenbush, S. W. (2005). Learning from attempts to improve schooling: The contribution of methodological diversity. *Educational Researcher, 34,* 25–31.

Reichle, E. D., Rayner, K., & Pollatsek, A. (2003). The E-Z reader model of eye-movement control in reading: comparisons to other models. *Behavioral and Brain Sciences, 26*(4), 445–476;

Ritter, S., Anderson, J. R., Koedinger, K. R., & Corbett, A. (2007). Cognitive tutor: Applied research in mathematics education. *Psychonomic Bulletin Review, 14,* 249–255.

Rychetnik, L., Frommier, M., Hawe, P., & Shiell, A. (2002). Criteria for evaluating evidence on public health interventions. *Journal of Epidemiology and Community Health, 56,* 119–127.

Shavelson, R. J., & Towne, L. (Eds.). (2002). *Scientific research in education.* Washington, DC: National Academies Press, National Research Council, Committee on Research on Education, Center for Education, Division of Behavioral and Social Sciences in Education.

Stokes, D. E. (1997). *Pasteur's quadrant: Basic science and technological innovation.* Washington, DC: Brookings Institution.

Toth, E. E., Klahr, D., & Chen, Z. (2000). Bridging research and practice: A cognitively based classroom intervention for teaching experimentation skills to elementary school children. *Cognition and Instruction, 18,* 423–459.

Towne, L., Wise, L., & Winters, T. (Eds.). (2005). *Advancing scientific research in education.* Washington, DC: National Academies Press, National Research Council, Committee on Research in Education, Center for Education, Division of Behavioral and Social Sciences in Education.

Van Lehn, K. (2006). The behavior of tutoring systems. *International Journal of Artificial Intelligence in Education, 16,* 227–265.

Van Lehn, K., Koedinger, K. R., Skogsholm, A., Nwaigwe, A., Hausmann, R. G. M., Weinstein, A., & Billings, B. (2007). Intelligent tutoring systems for continuous, embedded assessment. In C. A. Dwyer (Ed.), *The future of assessment: Shaping teaching and learning* (pp. 455–459). Mahwah, NJ: Erbaum.

Van Lehn, K., Lynch, C., Schulze, K., Shapiro, J., Shelby, R., Taylor, L., et al. (2005). The Andes Physics Tutoring System: Lessons learned. *International Journal of Artificial Intelligence in Education, 15*(3), 1–47.

Walker, E., Koedinger, K., McLaren, B., & Rummel, N. (2006). Cognitive tutors as research platforms: Extending an established tutoring system for collaborative and metacognitive experimentation. In M. Ikeda, K. Ashley, & T.-W. Chan (Eds.), *Intelligent tutoring systems 2006* (pp. 207–216). New York: Springer.

White, G., Frishkoff, G., & Bullock, M. (2008). Bridging the gap between psychological science and educational policy and practice. In K. T. C. Fiorello (Ed.), *Cognitive development in K–3 classroom learning: Research applications* (pp. 227–263). Mahwah, NJ: Erlbaum.

Whitehurst, G. (2003). *The Institute of Education Sciences: New wine, new bottles.* Retrieved on April 21, 2006 from http://www.ed.gov/rschstat/research/pubs/ies.html.

8

School Context and Microcontexts: The Complexity of Studying School Settings

Maria D. LaRusso, Joshua L. Brown,
Stephanie M. Jones, and J. Lawrence Aber

Researchers working at the intersection of education and psychology pursue a broad range of questions. Some focus on children; some on teachers and administrators; some on educational policies, curriculums, programs, or interventions; and others on the school context itself. Regardless of the specific research questions, what many of these investigations share in common is that they take place in schools. Even when researchers may not be interested in the school context as a focus of study, numerous studies have documented how features of school contexts can influence the educational and psychological processes and outcomes of students and staff, making school context a factor that must be considered in the design and implementation of any school-based study. This requires more than simply being conscious of the demographics of the school, as when researchers specify that a sample was obtained at large, urban high schools attended primarily by low-income students, with certain ratios of students from different racial or ethnic groups. It requires understanding that schools are systems made up of individuals (e.g., students, teachers, aides, and administrators) with their own characteristics and skills who both influence and are influenced by the complex set of microcontexts that exist in schools, each with its own social norms and supports.

At the very least, from an analytical standpoint, we know that studies conducted in schools must account for the influence of clustering, as in

This work was supported in part by a grant from the William T. Grant Foundation.

students within classrooms and classrooms within schools, and even sometimes schools within districts or regions. In the service of contributing to the practical knowledge of researchers who seek to conduct high-quality research in school environments, the specific goals of this chapter are to highlight the complexity and importance of school contexts, to provide an overview of the many ways in which we can assess and analyze school contexts, and to describe a number of practical issues in conducting research in and on school contexts.

IMPORTANCE AND COMPLEXITY OF SCHOOL CONTEXT AND MICROCONTEXTS

By examining several key features of school context that have demonstrated effects in previous psychological research, we highlight the complexity of what constitutes school context and why it warrants critical attention in school-based psychological and educational studies.

School Climate

Schools can differ in the quality of the school environment beyond demographic differences between schools, such as urban versus rural or suburban; compositional features, such as the socioeconomic status of the student population; or structural features, such as the availability of space and appropriate instructional materials. Specifically, the quality of the school environment can be operationalized to include factors such as violence and safety, disciplinary policies and rules, and the quality of relationships among students and staff. Studies have found school climate to have both direct and indirect effects on academic achievement (Anderson, 1982; Haynes, Emmons, & Ben-Avie, 1997); health risk behaviors, such as smoking, drinking, drug use, truancy, fighting, and weapon carrying (e.g., Catalano, Haggery, Oesterle, Fleming, & Hawkins, 2004); and mental health problems, such as symptoms of depression, anxiety, and suicidality (e.g., Kuperminc, Leadbeater, & Blatt, 2001). Specific components of school climate may be particularly important at certain ages. For example, research with adolescents has found that student autonomy, respect, and fair rules are negatively related to health risk behaviors at the school and/or individual level (e.g., LaRusso, Romer, & Selman, 2008; Samdal, Wold, Klepp, & Kannas, 2000; Welsh, 2001).

Climate of Classrooms and Other Microcontexts

There is typically greater variation in climate within schools than between schools. For example, students' perceptions of the quality of school climate vary more among students within the same school than between students from different schools (e.g., Brand, Felner, Shim, Seitsinger, & Dumas, 2003). Part of this is due to differences between classrooms and other microcontexts within schools. Elementary school children in the United States typically spend significant parts of their day in microcontexts other than their main classroom, including noninstructional settings such as lunchrooms and schoolyards, as well as settings in which they learn special subjects such as science, technology, library and research skills, physical education, and the arts. For children with learning disabilities or behavioral problems, sometimes more than half of the school day is spent in school microcontexts other than the main classroom, with different teachers and sometimes different peers. Furthermore, middle school and high school students typically experience even greater variation in microcontexts, because in addition to time spent in nonclassroom spaces like lunchrooms and gymnasiums, each academic subject is taught by a different teacher with different constellations of students.

Classrooms and microcontexts can vary in climate in ways that are important for psychological processes and outcomes. Positive classroom climate has been associated with greater self-esteem, perceived cognitive competence, internal locus of control, mastery motivation, school satisfaction, and academic performance, whereas lower quality classroom environments have been associated with poor peer relations, poor academic focus, and higher levels of aggression and other problem behaviors (e.g., Baker, 1999; Barth, Dunlap, Dane, Lochman, & Wells, 2004; R. M. Ryan & Grolnick, 1986; Toro et al., 1985). Although microcontexts other than the classroom have been studied less, research has identified certain microcontexts in schools to be unsafe, including hallways, lunchrooms, bathrooms, and playgrounds (Astor & Meyer, 2001), and studies across the world have found that bullying occurs most frequently on the playground (e.g., Meraviglia, Becker, Rosenbluth, Sanchez, & Robertson, 2003; Olweus, 1993). For school-based social and emotional learning or conflict resolution interventions, for example, it may be particularly important to assess change in such microcontexts.

Composition of School Context and Microcontexts

Schools and specific microcontexts within them are composed of both different teachers (with specific characteristics, skills, instructional styles, and levels of experience) and different combinations of students (each with their own social, emotional, and academic skills and behaviors). In addition to structural features related to composition, such as class size or adult–child ratios, teacher and student characteristics play an important role in educational contexts. Examples of teacher characteristics include their orientation toward their own professional development (e.g., Selman, 2003), their perceptions of their role in attending to students' social–emotional needs (e.g., A. M. Ryan, Gheen, & Midgley, 1998), their interest and ability in forming close relationships with their students (e.g., Hamre & Pianta, 2001), their experiences of stress and feelings of job burnout (e.g., Yoon, 2002), their classroom management styles and strategies (e.g., Wentzel, 2002), and their skill in promoting reading comprehension, word analysis, and writing skills (e.g., Rowan, Correnti, & Miller, 2002). Each of these has been identified as a critical dimension of teachers associated with the quality of teacher–student relationships and the development of children's social and/or academic competence.

Several studies have also identified child skills, beliefs, and behaviors that are associated with the quality of relationships and social interactions children experience in school. Children's behavioral orientations have an effect on the relationships formed with teachers and peers (e.g., Birch & Ladd, 1998). For example, children with overly aggressive interpersonal orientations may be avoided and thus grow increasingly isolated from positive classroom interactions (Wentzel, 1993). Similarly, students' normative beliefs about aggression also contribute to the relational climate of the classroom (Henry et al., 2000), and interventions intended to reduce hostile attribution bias are less effective when children are in classrooms in which aggression is considered acceptable behavior (Aber, Jones, Brown, Chaundry, & Samples, 1998).

School Context in Experimental Studies

Whether one is studying a school reform, a specific curriculum, or a behavioral intervention, the school context may be affected and may also moderate or mediate impacts on other outcomes. For example, the classroom environment has been shown to mediate the effect of teaching practices and programs on children's outcomes (e.g., Brock, Nishida, Chiong, Grimm, & Rimm-Kaufman, 2008; Kellam, Ling, Merisca, Brown, & Ialongo, 1998). Newly implemented programs may show no effects in some schools or classrooms while demonstrating effects in others. In such cases, it is possible that aspects of the school context can explain how or when a particular program may be more or less effective. In addition, many interventions profess a theory of change in which improved student outcomes are expected to be achieved through changing the quality of the classroom or the larger school environment. In these program evaluations, it is important to operationalize and measure these aspects of school context and include them in analyses both as direct outcomes and as mediators of change in student outcomes. Several evaluation studies have shown that school-based interventions may have positive effects on school climate (e.g., Cook, Murphy, & Hunt, 2000; Solomon, Watson, Battistich, & Schaps, 1996) and classroom climate (e.g., Brown, Jones, LaRusso, & Aber, 2008; Conduct Problems Prevention Research Group, 1999). Some evaluations of interventions have also examined changes in school microcontexts other than classrooms. For example, some studies demonstrated reductions in problem behaviors and increased use of negotiation strategies in microcontexts, such as hallways, the lunchroom, the playground, the gymnasium, and school entrances (e.g., Johnson, Johnson, Dudley, & Acikgoz, 1994; Lewis, Sugai, & Colvin, 1998). In sum, whether conducting descriptive or experimental studies in schools, it is essential that one understand the complexity of school contexts and microcontexts and their potential effects on psychological processes and outcomes.

CONCEPTUALIZATION, MEASUREMENT, AND ANALYSES OF SCHOOL CONTEXT AND MICROCONTEXTS

Our review of the literature suggests wide variation in the conceptualization and assessment of the school environment and its multiple microcontexts. Measurement of compositional features of school contexts typically consists of collecting data at the individual level, such as teacher and student characteristics like those described above, which can be aggregated to classroom and school levels. Assessments of the climate or environment of school contexts and microcontexts may utilize a range of data collection methods, including both quantitative and qualitative approaches. However, with the lack of a unifying framework or agreement on the dimensional structure, researchers are left to choose among not just a broad range of measures and methods but also a wide range of theoretical approaches and constructs. School climate ratings can also be analyzed at the level at which the data was collected (e.g., individual student level) or aggregated to the school level; however, it is important to keep in mind that, as previously mentioned, the majority of variation in school climate is within schools rather than between schools and aggregated scores would obscure the variation within schools.

Quantitative Methods

Quantitative approaches for assessing school climate most often use self-report measures. Most common are children's ratings (e.g., relationships with teachers, fairness of rules, safety) and teacher ratings (e.g., relationships with students, relationships with faculty and staff, aspects of the administrative climate). However, some studies have also utilized ratings by parents (e.g., perceptions of safety, parent–staff communication) and by other school personnel, such as cluster teachers and school aides. Some of these measures are constructed with parallel items and domains across reporters (e.g., student and teacher versions), whereas some school climate measures for teachers and staff focus more on the organizational climate of the school (e.g., collegiality, decision making). While researchers may use multi-informant assessments to create latent variables to approximate the "true" school climate, differences between the perspectives of, say, teachers and students may be substantively meaningful. A distinct value of these self-report measures is that how one perceives or directly experiences the climate of one's school may be as important as some objective measurement or average experience of school climate.

The constructs (or subscales) included in classroom and school climate measures also vary widely, and some measures do not differentiate among subscales at all, using instead one broad indicator of the quality of the school environment. More comprehensive measures may include 10 or more subscales (e.g., Brand et al., 2003). Some common domains in school climate measures include teacher support, clarity and consistency of rules, perceptions of safety, student autonomy, and participation in decision making. Although less common, some measures assess both positive and negative peer relations and factors that may be particularly relevant in diverse urban schools, such as support for cultural pluralism (e.g., Brand et al., 2003). However, even multidimensional school climate measures generally include broad items, such as "Teachers respect the students" or "There are a lot of fights in my school." When students have many teachers, particularly in the case of middle or high school, they may feel that some teachers are respectful and others are not, making such items difficult to answer and interpret. Similarly, students may report that there are, in fact, many fights but that these may occur only in the lunchroom; however, with most measures it is not possible to isolate the specific microcontexts that may be driving students' responses.

To date, the only measures of which we are aware that do begin to address these limitations are those that ask students to (a) identify specific school locations where they feel unsafe (e.g., hallways, bathroom, school entrances, classrooms) and (b) answer a group of items with a focus on one particular teacher or classroom (e.g., the English teacher or the first academic class after lunch period). This does increase specificity; however, in the first case, we are still limited to just one climate indicator (safety) for differentiating the environments of different microcontexts, and in the second case, we are obtaining specific climate information about only one microcontext. The reality is that this is a difficult issue to address in school climate questionnaires because asking students a battery of questions about each microcontext would potentially require a measure that would be too time intensive and costly to administer. Thus, this continues to be a limitation of student school climate questionnaires. Many of the measures available are homegrown assessments developed by schools or program developers, which can be appealing for the potential local relevance of included items but often lack necessary evidence of validity and reliability. Often the measures developed in research institutes and university settings are more adequate, having been subject to more rigorous analyses and measure refinement.

Quantitative approaches have also been used to assess classroom climate. Like school climate surveys, classroom climate assessments can include a wide range of dimensions, many of which are similar to school climate domains (e.g., rules, teacher support, peer relations) but are specific to the classroom (e.g., "Students in this class . . ." or "The teacher is . . ."). Some domains also tap instructional features of the classroom, like innovation (i.e., trying new things, encouraging creative thinking); however, certain aspects of instructional quality, such as concept development and quality of the teacher's feedback to students, are difficult to assess with self-report measures. These may be better assessed with structured observational tools, like the Classroom Assessment Scoring System (CLASS; see chap. 4, this volume).

Observational tools have also been utilized in microcontexts other than the classroom, such as behavioral checklists used in observations of children on playgrounds. These ratings are typically then used in qualitative analyses. Such ratings sometimes focus on the experiences of a specific child and other times aim to capture the environment more broadly. A limitation of the observational tools developed for playgrounds is that most focus solely on counts of problem behaviors. Because of the lack of available tools, little is known about how the broader climate (e.g., adult–child relationships, rules and approaches to behavior management, student autonomy) varies for school microcontexts beyond the classroom.

Qualitative Methods

Qualitative approaches can also be used to assess the quality of school contexts and microcontexts. A strength of these approaches is their ability to uncover the complexity, personal experiences, and meaning of social contexts. Particularly useful are individual or focus-group interviews with students, teachers, principals, school aides, and other staff. By using open-ended questions in interview settings, it is possible, for example, to obtain information about the processes that inform how individuals answer a survey question about how safe they feel in their school. One might learn that some adults in the school lack skills to help students resolve conflicts and even sometimes model aggressive behavior in their own interactions (e.g., LaRusso, Brown, Jones, & Aber, 2008). While focus group interviews are often thought of as an efficient way to collect several perspectives at once, the real benefits of this method for collecting contextual data are derived from the group process. Participants not only build on each other's responses but also interact in ways that reflect relationships and norms of social interaction that are typical of the setting (LaRusso & Selman, 2008). Group interviews can also be particularly useful in this regard. Unlike focus group interviews, group interviews involve several meetings over time which allow greater trust to be developed with the facilitator, topics to be discussed more deeply, and the group process to be observed more fully (LaRusso & Selman, 2008). Observational approaches are also a useful qualitative approach. Observations can be ethnographic in nature or utilize systematic rating systems (as described above). Ethnographic field notes obtained by observing a range of school settings can then be coded and used in cross-case analyses to identify salient patterns or differences among microcontexts or across schools. A distinct strength of ethnographic approaches is the possibility to uncover complex processes or to discover important contextual features of settings that would not be revealed by predefined scales or rating systems.

Mixed Methods

A few studies of school contexts and microcontexts have demonstrated the utility of mixed-method approaches (e.g., Feigenberg, 2008, LaRusso &

Selman, 2008) for capturing both general patterns within and between schools in perceptions of school climate while also uncovering the complexities that underlie these patterns. We used a mixed-method approach in our own research to examine the role of school contexts and microcontexts both in children's development and in the effectiveness of a school-based intervention. Using mixed methods, we were able to capitalize on existing, valid, and reliable measures of school contexts and to also move beyond the limitations of these measures with qualitative data that explore, for example, settings that are currently less well understood. In this cluster-randomized trial of a social–emotional and literacy program in 18 urban public elementary schools, we followed a cohort of students for 3 years and six waves of quantitative data collection that included measures of school climate, classroom climate, and teacher–student relationships. Four schools were also selected for in-depth study, stratified by treatment condition and student and teacher ratings of school climate quality. Qualitative data included ethnographic field notes from full-day observations in which groups of students were followed through the various settings of a typical day (e.g., classrooms, lunchrooms, playgrounds, hallways, gymnasiums), individual interviews with school staff, and student focus-group interviews. Staff interviews included a range of adults, including lunchroom aides, cluster teachers, and other school personnel who are typically not included in school-based research. These interviews illustrated how staff perceptions of the school context can vary extensively across schools (see Exhibit 8.1). Interviews with staff in various roles also provided insights into how microcontexts are perceived to be different both within and between schools (see Exhibit 8.2).

We were also able to examine variation between microcontexts with our focus groups. In particular, focus-group interviews utilized a mapping procedure (Astor et al., 2001) that asked students to examine maps of their schools and identify the microcontexts in which people get along well and/or in which there is a lot of conflict and problems getting along. As demonstrated in the examples provided in Figure 8.1, students experienced some microcontexts with primarily positive relationships (yellow stickers) and others with primarily negative relationships (green stickers). They also experienced settings in which both positive and negative

---

Exhibit 8.1

Perspectives of School Staff on School Context

The staff is great, um, you know they're close knit, we're all really in the same boat, learning a lot of new curriculums. I love the staff and the kids. You know, it's like, I wish there was more parental involvement, but the kids are *really* great kids, like you can tell who's been here from kindergarten to fifth grade, and you can tell who's new to this school, yeah, it's like a little community. And . . . I know when push comes to shove, the administration would definitely, you know, I think, back me, if there was something that was a problem.
—*Classroom teacher, School C*

A lot of the teachers are wonderful people and everybody tries very hard, but there's nothing fun, nice. You don't wake up in the morning: "can't wait to get to work." . . . This is a very hard place to work in. Lack of money, lack of background of the children . . . and the stress of having to educate them in a way that they can't possibly be educated. . . . The administration can't do much, they're totally overwhelmed. Um, it, it's very tough for them and therefore it's very tough for us . . . the administration can't help out, so you just do the best you can.
—*Classroom teacher, School B*

---

social interactions coexist (both yellow and green stickers in the same microcontext). The maps in Figure 8.1 were completed by a student in one of the schools with the most positive ratings of school climate; however, we can see that for this student there are many places where people do not get along well, like the schoolyard, gymnasium, a specific bathroom, and the child's own classroom. Thus, by integrating quantitative and qualitative data, we are able to begin to uncover some of the complexity of school settings that are not captured by existing measures or single data sources.

Exhibit 8.2

Perspectives of School Staff on School Microcontexts

I'll give you an example. One class in particular, and this is a kindergarten class, every time you go into this classroom, kids are sitting.
They are quiet. And you say, "Oh, what a nice class." The minute
they hit that cafeteria, it is on and popping. I got kids under the
table. I got kids running around. I got kids on top of the table. And
you would never know it is the same class, and it's the same kids.
—*Assistant principal/safety supervisor, School A*

[Fights usually occur in the] lunchroom, coming up stairs, to transition, recess, with a prep [cluster] teacher. Never usually when
there are teachers around, the real teacher.
—*Classroom teacher, School C*

We have a lot of fights right within the classroom, some in lunch,
um mostly within the classroom. Which really shows that they're
really not paying attention to what's being taught . . . because their
mind is someplace else.
—*Assistant principal, School B*

[The people who run the lunchroom and the kindergarten class-
rooms] are not good in discipline. They're weak on that . . . knowing what to say, what to do, what not to do. . . . Kindergarten and
the cafeteria are out of control for the most part. Unless the principal goes in there to hold them down, you know the cafeteria is
going to be full of fights.
—*Technology teacher, School B*

It depends on the management style. I think that it's all about
management and I see that many of our real behavior problems
that are containable in their classroom, they go to clusters and they
fall apart. So we try to put strong teachers in as cluster teachers.
Sometimes you're successful at that, sometimes you're not.
—*Assistant principal/special education supervisor, School A*

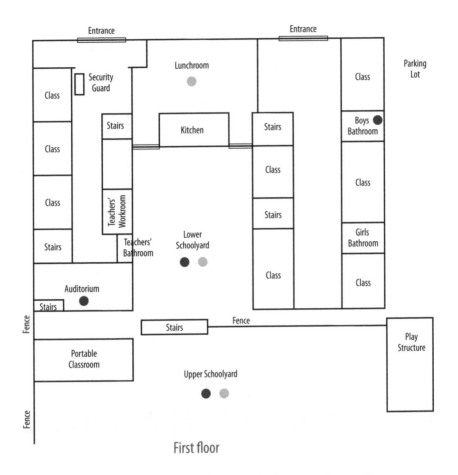

First floor

● Places where people *do not* get along well

● Places where people get along well

Figure 8.1

Sample Student Completed Map From School C.

(continued)

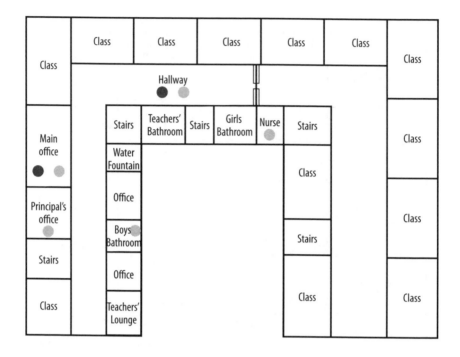

Second floor

Figure 8.1

Sample Student Completed Map From School C. *(Continued)*

Analytical Issues

Lastly, several design and methodological considerations are important in studying school contexts. First, because of the nested and interrelated nature of these contexts, analyses must always take clustering into account. Multilevel modeling techniques allow one to decompose variance into its individual (e.g., within-classrooms and schools) and group (e.g., between-classrooms and schools) components, and standard errors are appropriately adjusted for nonindependence due to the clustering of data (Bryk & Raudenbush, 1992). A typical multilevel model would have data on individual students at Level 1, with classroom-level (or other school microcontext) data (e.g., cafeteria, schoolyard), including teacher characteristics,

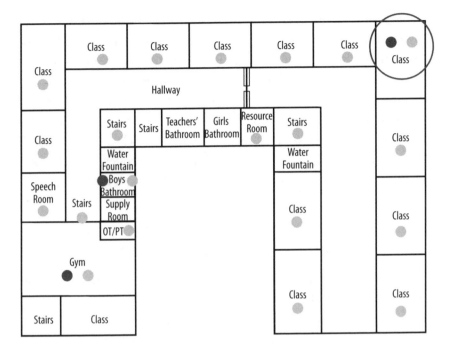

Third floor
(child's main classroom is circled)

Figure 8.1

Sample Student Completed Map From School C. *(Continued)*

at Level 2, and school-level data at Level 3 (e.g., school demographics, such as urban vs. rural, public vs. private, poverty levels). It is also possible to aggregate data from one level to a higher level as another way to examine setting level characteristics (e.g., individual student behavioral problems aggregated to the classroom level as a measure of the degree of behavioral disorder in the classroom). This requires consideration not just of average aggregated scores but also indices of variation (e.g., extent of variation in individual student behavioral problems in the classroom rather than just the average level). Middle and high schools are especially complicated when it comes to clustering. Composition of the classroom, including both teachers and students, typically changes from one period to the next, so that it often is not possible to model clustering at the classroom level. This is also a problem in longitudinal studies in elementary schools because classroom clustering often changes from year to year. Thus, alternative approaches need to be used, such as classroom clustered within-year analyses or cross-classified models in which individual change is modeled based on patterns of cross-year classroom membership. Another possibility is the use of piecewise models that estimate the influence of classroom context in 1 year on individual-level change over that and subsequent years in combination with the influence of each successive classroom context.

CONDUCTING RESEARCH IN SCHOOL CONTEXTS: PRACTICAL CONSIDERATIONS

Features of school contexts can also influence the quality of data collected in school-based studies. In particular, constraints and characteristics of the school context determine who will be included in the study, how participants are clustered, and the quality of school climate data.

Variations in Composition

The composition of classrooms and other microcontexts can vary according to the type of setting, time of day, disciplinary actions, and natural fluctuations in the school population. Which students will be included in classroom-based data collection may depend on the type of classroom. In middle and high schools, composition of classrooms often varies due to ability-based tracking of students. Staff and student composition also vary in elementary schools where there are several kinds of main classrooms, including those that are team taught, multigrade, gifted and talented, special education, or that include paraprofessionals to support students with disabilities.

Regardless of the type of main classroom, the students will also pass through a variety of microcontexts in their day, and features of these microcontexts also vary. In elementary schools, for example, composition of students will be different in the lunchroom and schoolyard versus in the primary classroom. The times when students are in these areas are often the times of day when students have the most contact with peers outside their main classroom, frequently including peers from different grades. Whereas typically there are school aides with the specific job of supervising students in the lunchroom and playground, at some schools parent volunteers, principals, or disciplinary deans also perform these duties. Particularly in schools that are understaffed for lunch and recess, paraprofessionals may assist with supervision and older students sometimes provide support as "monitors" of younger students. Lunch and recess are also sometimes organized in split periods, so that the specific staff members will vary depending on whether students have lunch first or recess first.

Composition of school settings can also vary according to the time of day. For example, in high schools, some students may be present in the school only for the early part of the day, leaving early each day to attend vocational technical programs off-site. In elementary schools, there are also parts of the day when students will be in their main classroom, but the composition of the classroom may be atypical (e.g., several students leave to receive special services or for band practice). And particularly important for collecting observational data, there are times when an adult other than the primary classroom teacher (e.g., a student teacher or a literacy specialist) may be teaching or cofacilitating the class.

Schools generally have different disciplinary codes and policies that can also affect who is present during data collection. In some middle and high schools, students are regularly sent to the main office because of rule infractions or disciplined with in-school suspension that may reduce the presence of the higher risk students in their classrooms during periods of data collection. In elementary schools, disruptive children are frequently sent to a neighboring classroom for a period of time, presumably to give both the teacher and student time apart. Thus, classroom observers often encounter students from other classrooms who are temporarily visiting the classroom being observed but are not normally members of that classroom. One way of examining context is aggregating individual characteristics or skills to the context level. For example, we might aggregate students' beliefs about aggression to the classroom level as a measure of the aggressive orientation of the classroom. In cases such as this, it is important to obtain data from as many students in the classroom as possible, and we especially do not want to be missing data from students with behavioral problems.

Who participates in data collection is also affected by common fluctuations in the school population. Student absenteeism is an unavoidable problem that affects who is present on any given day for data collection. Particularly, when collecting student survey data, plans can be made for additional visits to have these students complete the surveys. Often this requires multiple visits and one-to-one sessions with students and should be planned into research budgets. In addition, longitudinal studies will be confronted with a variety of issues related to retention. Especially in low-income, urban schools, mobility rates can be quite high for both teachers and students. This means both losses of participants and gains of many new participants each year, requiring new rounds of consenting, potentially at each new wave of data collection.

Collecting Climate Data

Collecting school climate data presents some particular challenges. When asking staff and students to share their perspectives on school climate in either surveys or interviews, issues of privacy and confidentiality may be particularly important. Typically, research staff are not legally authorized to be alone with students so that even when conducting group administrations of surveys with entire classrooms of students, the teacher or another school staff member needs to be present. This can be tricky in elementary schools when group administrations often are conducted with research staff reading each question aloud and questions include ratings of aspects of school climate, such as perceptions of teachers and student–teacher relationships. It can be uncomfortable for research staff and teachers alike when an item that asks, for example, about the extent of teacher's respect for students is met by groans from responding students. When surveys include climate questions, the ideal scenario would be to administer surveys in the presence of a school adult who plays a less central role in the students' school lives. While this may be impossible for logistical reasons, it both allows the students greater privacy and comfort in answering sensitive questions and can help to preserve the relationship between the research team and the teachers. This can be even more important when conducting individual or focus-group interviews with students who may be disinclined to speak candidly about their school relationships and experiences without adequate privacy.

School personnel can also be hesitant to share their perspectives on school climate, even if confidentiality is promised. Often the questionnaires ask school staff to identify their role in the school, and it is common that there is only one physical education teacher, for example, making an individual's identity evident even without the use of names in analyses or reports. In addition, nontenured teachers and school staff in the positions with the least power may be the most hesitant to participate because of concerns about job security. For example, in our own research, it was particularly difficult to find lunch aides who were willing to participate in interviews and even more so in schools where there seemed to be tensions with or mistrust of the administration.

Timing of data collection can also affect the quality of school climate data. When collecting climate data, it is better to avoid the first 4 to 6 weeks of school, when patterns of interaction and perceptions of the environment are still developing. Also, classroom and school climate studies have identified fluctuations that are typical across the school year. Both school climate and certain domains of classroom climate have been found to decline over the course of the school year (e.g., Gest, Welsh, & Domitrovich, 2005; see also chap. 4, this volume). These patterns are particularly important for longitudinal and experimental studies. The timing of data collection will matter. When evaluating an intervention using climate indicators, it would be important to be consistent in the timing of data collection from year to year and between intervention and control schools.

SUMMARY

When conducting psychological research in the natural setting of schools, context is a factor that must be considered in both study design and implementation. An extensive literature documents the importance of several features of the school context for children and adolescent's social–emotional and academic development. The complexity of school settings is evident in the many ways that researchers have developed to conceptualize and measure the school context and its many microcontexts. Despite current limitations, this is a burgeoning field that includes both a broad repertoire of established tools and new methods of assessment and analysis that are constantly emerging. Our understanding of both developmental pathways and the impact of programs and interventions will be enhanced by including assessments of critical features of school context in our school-based studies. In addition, implementation of any study within school settings requires an understanding of the processes and norms that define school systems. Taking into account the school context and all of its complexities not only makes us better researchers but also makes us better partners in working with schools.

REFERENCES

Aber, J. L., Jones, S. M., Brown, J. L., Chaudry, N., & Samples, F. (1998). Resolving conflict creatively: Evaluating the developmental effects of a school-based violence prevention program in neighborhood and classroom context. *Development and Psychopathology, 10*, 187–213.

Anderson, C. S. (1982). The search for school climate: A review of the research. *Review of Educational Research, 52*, 368–420.

Astor, R. A., & Meyer, H. A. (2001). The conceptualization of violence-prone school subtexts: Is the sum of the parts greater than the whole? *Urban Education, 36*, 372–399.

Astor, R. A., Meyer, H. A., & Pitner, R. O. (2001). Elementary and middle school students' perceptions of violence-prone school subcontexts. *The Elementary School Journal, 101*, 511–528.

Baker, J. A. (1999). Teacher–student interaction in urban at-risk classrooms: Differential behavior, relationship quality, and student satisfaction with school. *The Elementary School Journal, 100*, 57–70.

Barth, J. M., Dunlap, S. T., Dane, H., Lochman, J. E., & Wells, K. C. (2004). Classroom environment influences on aggression, peer relations, and academic focus. *Journal of School Psychology, 42*, 115–133.

Birch, S. H., & Ladd, G. W. (1998). Children's interpersonal behaviors and the teacher–child relationship. *Developmental Psychology, 34*, 934–946.

Brand, S., Felner, R., Shim, M., Seitsinger, A., & Dumas, T. (2003). Middle school improvement and reform: Development and validation of a school-level assessment of climate, cultural pluralism, and school safety. *Journal of Educational Psychology,* 95, 570–588.

Brock, L., Nishida, T., Chiong, C., Grimm, K., & Rimm-Kaufman, S. (2008). Children's perceptions of the classroom environment and social and academic performance: A longitudinal analysis of the contribution of the responsive classroom approach. *Journal of School Psychology, 46,* 129–149.

Brown, J. L., Jones, S. M., LaRusso, M. D., & Aber, J. L. (under review). Improving classroom quality: Teacher influences and experimental impacts of the 4Rs Program. *Journal of Educational Psychology.*

Bryk, A. S., & Raudenbush, S. W. (1992). *Hierarchical linear models: Applications and data analysis methods.* Newbury Park, CA: Sage.

Catalano, R. F., Haggery, K. P., Oesterle, S., Fleming, C. B., & Hawkins, J. D. (2004). The importance of bonding to school for healthy development: Findings from the Social Development Research Group. *Journal of School Health, 74,* 252–261.

Conduct Problems Prevention Research Group. (1999). Initial impact of the Fast Track Prevention Trial for Conduct Problems: II. Classroom effects. *Journal of Consulting and Clinical Psychology, 67,* 648–657.

Cook, T. D., Murphy, R. F., & Hunt, D. H. (2000). Comer's school development program in Chicago: A theory-based evaluation. *American Educational Research Journal, 37,* 535–597.

Feigenberg, L. (2008, March). *The influence of school climate on students' behavior and social development: A mixed-methods study.* Paper presented at the annual meeting of the American Educational Research Association, New York, NY.

Gest, S. D., Welsh, J. A., & Domitrovich, C. E. (2005). Behavioral predictors of changes in social relatedness and liking school in elementary school. *Journal of School Psychology, 43,* 281–301.

Hamre, B. K., & Pianta, R. C. (2001). Early teacher–child relationships and the trajectory of children's school outcomes through eighth grade. *Child Development, 72,* 625–638.

Haynes, N. M., Emmons, C., & Ben-Avie, M. (1997). School climate as a factor in student adjustment and achievement. *Journal of Educational and Psychological Consultation, 8,* 321–329.

Henry, D., Guerra, N., Huesmann, R., Tolan, P., VanAcker, R., & Eron, L. (2000). Normative influences on aggression in urban elementary school classrooms. *American Journal of Community Psychology, 28,* 59–81.

Johnson, D. W., Johnson, R., Dudley, B., & Acikgoz, K. (1994). Effects of conflict resolution training on elementary students. *Journal of Social Psychology, 134,* 803–817.

Kellam, S. G., Ling, X., Merisca, R., Brown, C. H., & Ialongo, N. (1998). The effect of the level of aggression in the first grade classroom on the course and malleability of aggressive behavior into middle school. *Development and Psychopathology, 10,* 165–186.

Kuperminc, G. P., Leadbeater, B. J., & Blatt, S. J. (2001). School social climate and individual differences in vulnerability to psychopathology among middle school students. *Journal of School Psychology, 39,* 141–159.

LaRusso, M. D., Brown, J. L., Jones, S. M., & Aber, J. L. (2008, July). *Aggressive behavior in elementary schools in the United States: Links to school climate, relationships, and responses to aggression.* Poster session presented at the biennial meeting of the International Society for the Study of Behavioral Development, Würzburg, Germany.

LaRusso, M. D., Romer, D., & Selman, R. L. (2008). Teachers as builders of respectful school climates: Implications for adolescent drug use norms and depressive symptoms in high school. *Journal of Youth and Adolescence, 37,* 386–398.

LaRusso, M. D., & Selman, R. L. (2008). *Students' social awareness and the middle school climate: Implications for risk behaviors and cynical attitudes toward school based prevention initiatives.* Manuscript submitted for publication.

Lewis, T. J., Sugai, G., & Colvin, G. (1998). Reducing problem behavior through a school-wide system of effective behavioral support: Investigation of a school-wide social skills training program and contextual interventions. *School Psychology Review, 27,* 446–459.

Meraviglia, M. G., Becker, H., Rosenbluth, B., Sanchez, E., & Robertson, T. (2003). The Expect Respect Project: Creating a positive elementary school climate. *Journal of Interpersonal Violence, 18,* 1347–1360.

Olweus, D. (1993). Children on playgrounds: The role of victimization. In C. H. Hart (Ed.), *Children on playgrounds: Research perspectives and applications* (pp. 85–128). Albany: State University of New York Press.

Rowan, B., Correnti, R., & Miller, R. J. (2002). *What large-scale survey research tells us about teacher effects on student achievement: Insights from the Prospects study of elementary schools* (CPRE Research Report Series No. RR051). Philadelphia: Consortium for Policy Research in Education, University of Pennsylvania, Graduate School of Education.

Ryan, A. M., Gheen, M. H., & Midgley, C. (1998). Why do some students avoid asking for help? An examination of the interplay among students' academic efficacy, teachers' social–emotional role, and the classroom goal structure. *Journal of Educational Psychology, 88,* 1–8.

Ryan, R. M., & Grolnick, W. S. (1986). Origins and pawns in the classroom: Self-report and projective assessments of individual differences in children's perceptions. *Journal of Personality and Social Psychology, 50,* 550–558.

Samdal, O., Wold, B., Klepp, K. I., & Kannas, L. (2000). Students' perceptions of school and their smoking and alcohol use: A cross-national study. *Addiction Research, 8,* 141–167.

Selman, R. L. (2003). *The promotion of social awareness: Powerful lessons from the partnership of developmental theory and classroom practice.* New York: Russell Sage Foundation.

Solomon, D., Watson, M., Battistich, V., & Schaps, E. (1996). Creating classrooms that students experience as communities. *American Journal of Community Psychology, 24,* 719–748.

Toro, P. A., Cowen, E. L., Gesten, E. L., Weissberg, R. P., Rapkin, B. D., & Davidson, E. (1985). Social environmental predictors of children's adjustment in elementary school classrooms. *American Journal of Community Psychology, 13,* 353–364.

Welsh, W. N. (2001). Effects of student and school factors on five measures of school disorder. *Justice Quarterly, 18,* 911–947.

Wentzel, K. R. (1993). Does being good make the grade? Social behavior and academic competence in middle school. *Journal of Educational Psychology, 85,* 357–364.

Wentzel, K. R. (2002). Are effective teachers like good parents? Teaching styles and student adjustment in early adolescence. *Child Development, 73,* 287–301.

Yoon, J. S. (2002). Teacher characteristics as predictors of teacher–student relationships: Stress, negative affect, and self-efficacy. *Social Behavior and Personality, 30,* 485–493.

9

Disseminating Scholarship to Diverse Audiences

Amy Bellmore and Sandra Graham

Given the inherent relevance of educational research for children's lives, educational researchers are in a unique position to influence theory, policy, and practice through their scholarship (Higgins-D'Alessandro & Jankowski, 2002). Although most scholars of educational and developmental processes set out to address primarily theoretical concerns and view other scholars as their target audience, we argue that findings garnered from educational research should be shared with both scholarly and general audiences. Because the approach that will be most successful for one audience may not work well with other audiences, in this chapter, we describe a range of methods for disseminating educational research findings to diverse audiences.

We have identified three core audiences that can benefit from the results yielded by school-based scholarship. The first audience consists of scholars from disciplines that are concerned with the welfare of children. Here we focus on the fields of psychology, education, and child development. Within academia, the scholarly audience is highly valued and, as such, much empirical research may not extend beyond the format of refereed journals (McCall, 1996). While this audience is significant because members can effectively evaluate the merits of the scholarship and extend on it to yield new findings, equally valuable are audiences that can directly

We would like to thank Carmen De La Cruz, Suzanne Markoe, and Fernando Bibian for their valuable contributions to this chapter.

benefit from the scholarship by using it to implement changes in their lives. With this in mind, we view the second key audience as those who work in professional settings addressing educational issues. This audience comprises practitioners such as teachers, principals, and other school staff members and extends to policymakers who influence educational practices through legislative means. The third core audience is composed of the study participants. Depending on the nature of the study, this group might include student, teacher, staff, and parent participants. These individuals should be recognized as the key stakeholders in the research process because their lives are immediately affected by participating in the study and because the findings generated by the research are most relevant to their school community.

Given that each audience has a unique vantage point in the research process, there are differences in how each audience can best be reached. For example, teachers and parents may not have access to academic journals nor would they necessarily look to such sources when seeking information. Suggestions for navigating these differences are discussed below.

There are also important similarities between the audiences. First, our use of the term *audience* is not meant to imply that the target recipients of the information play a passive role. In fact, in our discussion below we emphasize methods for facilitating access for individuals, such as parents or policymakers, who actively seek out information related to educational processes. Second, we hope that widespread dissemination will help to expand the audience of scholarship by creating a general public that is ready to critically evaluate messages about education with the same toolbox that educational researchers use.

Because the publication of empirical studies published in academic journals is a highly valued outlet for scholars of educational processes, we used this as a starting point for our chapter. We first examined the breadth of the dissemination of empirical findings obtained in school settings to other scholars through publication in academic journals. Specifically, we examined the proportion of empirical studies that were conducted within school settings that were published since the year 2000 within three major journals from the fields of psychology, education, and child development. We also determined the proportion of these school-based studies that included an experimental component within the study. To do so, we looked for studies that randomly assigned individuals to a treatment group or to a control group to measure the effects of a given treatment. We chose this as an important feature of the studies because there is a growing emphasis on the implementation of evidence-based educational practices stemming from the No Child Left Behind (NCLB) Act of 2001 (Public Law 107-110). NCLB calls on individuals to rely on the most rigorous scientifically based information, such as those that use randomized controlled trials, to improve U.S. educational practices (Coalition for Evidence-Based Policy, 2003). Thus, this analysis of recently published studies was designed to inform us about the extent to which researchers are conducting the types of investigations that are valued by policymaking and grant-providing organizations within the United States.

Because there is no clear-cut way to quantify the amount of scholarship that is disseminated to practitioners, policymakers, and stakeholders, we took a different approach in the second half of the chapter. To encourage scholars to disseminate their findings more broadly, we reviewed a range of formats that can be used to target these audiences. Recognizing the importance of preserving the message across formats, we highlight how slight shifts in the presentation of the message increases the accessibility and potential influence of the message. For each format, we described why it should be effective for a particular audience, the potential benefits of using the format, and whether there are resources available to scholars hoping to utilize the format.

REACHING SCHOLARS OF EDUCATIONAL PROCESSES

To establish the extent to which school-based empirical studies have been published within three fields where educational research is conducted, we chose one major research outlet published by the professional organization representing the fields of psychology, education, and child development. A common characteristic of the professional organizations that we chose is that each represents the interests of both scholars and practitioners. For psychology, we chose the *Journal of Educational Psychology*, which is published by the American Psychological Association (APA). For education, we chose the *American Educational Research Journal,* which is published by the American Educational Research Association (AERA). To represent the field of child development, we chose *Child Development,* which is a major research outlet of the Society for Research on Child Development (SRCD). The specific missions and goals of each journal are described below. We analyzed these journals separately because they differ on such characteristics as publication frequency, editorial periods, and content emphases, making them not directly comparable.

Because we were interested in current trends within these journals, we limited our analysis to the years 2000 to 2006. For these years, we examined the method section of every original empirical article examining children and adolescents who were in any grade between kindergarten and 12th grade. A study was included if the participants were in any of these grades at any time during the course of the study. For example, longitudinal studies that predicted elementary school functioning from preschool measures were included, as were longitudinal studies that predicted adult functioning from school-age functioning. In addition to excluding studies that examined only children younger than kindergarten age and beyond high school age, we excluded all reviews, theoretical overviews, commentaries, and essays.

Once we established this article base, we coded two aspects of the studies. First, we assessed whether the study was conducted within a school setting for any part of the data collection. We deemed these studies "school-based studies." To qualify as a school-based study, school participation needed to have been explicitly described as active involvement of school personnel in data collection (e.g., as part of regular lessons), the provision of space within the school for carrying out the study (e.g., classrooms or hallways), or the inclusion of school-affiliated informants such as teachers or peers (e.g., teacher ratings). There was no restriction on the type of school setting; private and public schools were included as were those identified as serving special populations such as deaf children.

Next, we further analyzed those studies that were defined as school based to determine whether an experimental method was used for any part of the study. Those studies that explicitly mentioned the use of an experimental method or the use of control and treatment groups were designated as experiments. The experimental method could exist at the level of the schools, classrooms, teachers, or students. For example, an investigation of the effects of class size on student academic performance would compare classrooms with one another, whereas an investigation of word learning might compare students with one another. We reviewed the data generated from these analyses below separately for each journal. We then commented on general trends across all three journals and offer suggestions for effective practices for disseminating school-based empirical findings in academic journals.

The official description of the *Journal of Educational Psychology* states that it "publishes original, primary psychological research pertaining to education across all ages and educational levels" (http://www.apa.org/journals/edu/description.html). Our analysis revealed that 61% of the articles published between 2000 and 2006 examined a K–12 population within an empirical study. Of the 278 K–12 empirical studies, 71% were school based. Of the 196 school-based studies, 27% ($n = 53$) used an experimental methodology.

The *American Educational Research Journal* "publishes original empirical and theoretical studies and analyses in education" (http://aerj.aera.net). The journal is divided into two sections: the Teaching, Learning, and Human Development section and the Social and Institutional Analysis section. We analyzed articles from both sections because each publishes empirical studies that fit our criteria. Our analysis revealed that 73% of the articles published between 2000 and 2006 examined a K–12 population within an empirical study. Of the 141 K–12 empirical studies, 89% were school based. Of the 126 school-based studies, only 10% ($n = 13$) used experimental methodology. Thus, although school-based studies were predominant in this journal, few utilized experimental methods.

The third journal, *Child Development,* publishes "original contributions on topics in child development from the fetal period through adolescence" (http://www.srcd.org/cd.html). Our analysis revealed that 59% of the articles examined a K–12 population within the context of an empirical study. Of the 416 K–12 empirical studies, 57% were school based. Of the 237 school-based studies, 27% ($n = 63$) were experimental.

Across the three journals, the publication trends suggest that comparatively little research conducted with children and adolescents between the years 2000 and 2006 was experimental research conducted within school contexts. As shown in Figure 9.1, across the journals, only between 5% and 10% of these studies were classified as such. These small percentages are somewhat surprising given the recent push for evidence-based educational practices (Coalition for Evidence-Based Policy, 2003). It will be interesting to follow whether there is an increase in school-based experimental studies in the coming years or whether such an increase plays out more in some journals than others. Evaluating such trends can inform us about the impact of policy changes on scholarship about educational practices, which in turn should extend to new or modified policies and practices.

Attending to current trends in topics and methods in educational research is also important for individual scholars as they make decisions about what types of research questions to address, what methods to use,

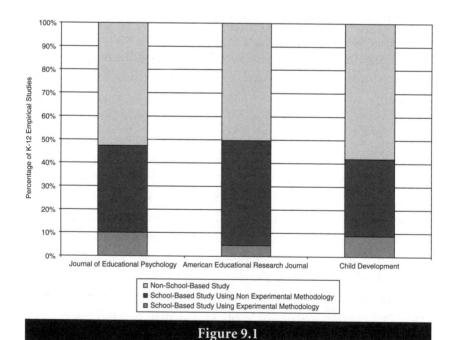

Figure 9.1

Percentage of empirical articles published from 2000 to 2006 including K–12 participants using three different methodologies.

and where to publish. There are numerous important scholarly journals that are read by teacher education faculty such as the *Journal of Mathematics Education* and *Reading Research Quarterly*. Although we did not review the publishing trends in these journals, it is important to note that these venues may be particularly attractive publishing outlets. By targeting teacher education faculty, these venues may provide the first step in the implementation of effective educational methods.

Beyond content, another important aspect of dissemination that scholars should consider is *when* to publish their findings in journals. This is especially important for scholars examining developmental processes longitudinally across school years. Scholars face a balancing act between sharing their findings and holding off long enough to tell a complete story. They also need to be concerned about the pitfalls of piecemeal publishing, which can happen when a series of studies is published from the same sample and data set, with only trivial differences between them. In our own longitudinal school-based research on adolescents across grades 6 through 12 (Bellmore, Witkow, Graham, & Juvonen, 2004), we have worked to release the findings from our study methodically so that we are telling a story that continues to build on itself.

EFFECTIVE OUTLETS FOR PRACTITIONERS, POLICYMAKERS, AND STAKEHOLDERS

The significance of using empirical findings as a basis for practice has been identified as a key challenge faced by both scholars and practitioners (Fisher, 1993). One way for scholars to meet this challenge is to work actively to disseminate their findings to practitioners, policymakers, the general public, and research participants. In this way, their findings can form the basis for new educational practices, policies, and funding initiatives with the end goal of benefiting students.

A starting place for identifying outlets that target general audiences is to consider the opportunities available through the professional organizations identified above. Each organization has different means for facilitating communications with the public, media, and policymakers (Maton & Bishop-Josef, 2006). For example, APA has a public policy office (http://www.apa.org/ppo) that links psychologists to federal agencies and legislators as well as Web-based information and resources for the general public on hot topics in psychology (http://www.apa.org/topics). AERA has a communications staff that connects researchers and news media to facilitate coverage of educational issues (http://www.aera.net). They also publish a quarterly series, *Research Points*, which describes current research relevant for educational policymakers.

As part of its current strategic plan, SRCD emphasizes "its dissemination of research-based knowledge to inform research priorities, public policy, professional and educational practice, and the broader public" (McCabe, 2005, p. 2). As such, SRCD facilitates connections between researchers and the general public by requiring authors of articles published in *Child Development* to write a public summary and by issuing press releases for selected research published in the journal likely to be of high interest to the public. They also support an Office for Policy and Communications, which publishes a *Social Policy Report Brief* four times a year to provide both policymakers and SRCD membership with objective reviews of research findings on topics of national interest and current policy issues.

REACHING GENERAL AUDIENCES

Given the variety in possible audiences, it is important for scholars to consider which methods of dissemination will be most effective for each audience. Differing methods may emphasize communicating a general message to many people or a more specific message to a few people. Thus, it is critical for scholars to match their goals with their methods (McCall & Groark, 2000). In this section, we review several options, starting with those formats that have the potential for the broadest impact.

Utilize Communications Staff

Communicating with the general public through media outlets such as television, radio, and newspapers provides opportunities to reach large numbers of the public. Scholars may be contacted when current events warrant their expertise, but they may also seek out opportunities to share their work with the public. Because this approach requires access and particular communication techniques, it is helpful to partner with a professional who can translate your findings to the media. Universities, professional organizations, and granting agencies often have public relations staff that can provide practice opportunities, help scholars prepare press releases, and ensure that the message is balanced between accurately representing results and being newsworthy enough to capture the interests of the public. Groark and McCall (2005) discussed what types of research makes the news and provided specific tips for scholars utilizing the media to share their findings.

Benefits of this approach include providing answers to questions currently faced by the public, raising issues that the public may not yet be aware of, and facilitating the expansion of specific research areas by demonstrating a need for public funding. However, scholars should be aware that, in contrast to publication of journal articles, they have less control over how and where the message is communicated by the media and how it is interpreted by the public (Groark & McCall, 2005).

Write Op-Ed Pieces on Timely Topics

Writing an op-ed (opinion-editorial) piece is another way to reach the public. Authors usually have a better chance of getting an op-ed piece published if they write about current events and target local outlets for publication. In addition, individuals who can demonstrate an expertise in a given area are more likely to be published. This format therefore provides a perfect opportunity for scholars of educational processes to introduce their knowledge into public discourse when a topic in the news relates to their body of research. This approach can be very effective because it provides a format for sharing important perspectives that may be missing from general public discussions about the topic of interest. It should be noted that op-ed pieces represent a different genre of writing than what most of us practice in our scholarly work for peer review. In relatively few words and with very little lead time, the author must analyze the strengths and weaknesses of the current educational practice under consideration and advocate for particular solutions based on a persuasive synthesis of the research. We encourage scholars who are considering the op-ed as a dissemination outlet to seek out workshops at their institutions that provide training in this genre.

Foster Relations With Local, State, and Federal Policymakers

Although the divide between scholarship and policymaking is wide (Shonkoff, 2000), communicating with policymakers is the best way to ensure that scholarship is used as the basis for solving real-world issues. One route to influencing policy work is to provide a briefing paper to policymakers looking for experts in certain areas.

Usually no more than one page in length, briefing papers identify a problem and a solution offered by the scholar's work (Groark & McCall, 2005). In such cases, the message shared by the scholar is not modified, and the ideas in the briefing paper relate directly to current issues within society. Briefing papers differ from other scholarly reports in that they must be concise and detailed. Moreover, the time scale differs from the normal path of scholarship because needs often arise suddenly, and solutions are required immediately. The importance of timing for effectively introducing developmental scholarship into the policy process is a theme echoed frequently by those who have examined the translation of research into policy (Groark & McCall, 2005; Mahoney & Zigler, 2006).

Produce or Contribute to Practice-Oriented Web Sites

Using the Internet is a cost-effective venue with the potential to reach a large audience (Rothbaum, Martland, & Bishop-Josef, 2007). There are several ways to best make use of the Internet as a dissemination method. Scholars can produce a Web site that contains the questions they are working to address, findings from their body of research to date, and links to other relevant Web-based content. A benefit of producing a Web site is that the owner is able to control the accuracy of the information posted. However, scholars who wish to post electronic versions of their publications on their own Web sites are cautioned to do so within the specific guidelines outlined by the original publisher of the work. A different approach to using the Internet as a dissemination method is to contribute to an already existing forum that reaches a broad spectrum of the lay public.

A new Internet format that seeks to link the design of educational inter-ventions, the evaluation of interventions, and the public's access to this information is the What Works Clearinghouse sponsored by the U.S. Department of Education's Institute of Education Sciences (http://ies.ed.gov/ncee/wwc). Established in 2002, this Web site provides reviews of promis-ing educational programs. Anyone is permitted to submit intervention studies to be critically evaluated for their effectiveness by expert reviewers. On the basis of a review of all submitted and identified high-quality exper-imental studies on a given topic, the Web site provides a report that can be utilized by anyone looking for information on that topic.

In addition to potentially having virtually no boundaries to who may access the work, Web sites often also provide opportunities for scholars to hear from those who visit the site. For example, visitors might e-mail scholars or might make comments in a discussion area of the site. Both of these provide feedback to scholars that may shape their future theoretical and empirical work.

Organize Symposia Around Relevant Issues

An effective method for reaching practitioners is to organize symposia around hot topics at national, university-sponsored, or community-based conferences. When we have participated in such venues, practitioners have responded favorably to research-based content. Moreover, the inter-active nature of the sessions has provided immediate feedback to us about the relevance of our work. Such sessions also have sparked new ideas for future research from those working on the front lines. However, whereas other approaches described earlier have the potential to reach many people, the direct impact of symposia is usually limited to those practitioners seeking out specific information.

BENEFITING STAKEHOLDERS

Presumably, school-based research is motivated by the desire to improve the well-being of children who spend a good deal of their time in educa-tional settings. It is therefore incumbent on researchers to inform students, parents, and teachers about what the research reveals about child well-being. Dissemination to stakeholders can provide insight into practices that work and those that do not or that may even be harmful, can dispel myths that have no basis in sound research, and can generate excitement about innovative new practices.

Conduct Workshops for Participating Students, School Personnel, and Parents

Scholars should grab opportunities to interact directly with participants via workshops or presentations at local schools in which they conduct their research. Effective venues include giving in-service school or staff trainings or presentations at parent night meetings. Usually, scholars can tie their own research directly to topics of interest to a specific school community. Such presentations may function similarly to practitioner-focused symposia as described above, but an added component is the ability to offer solutions to specific problems faced in a given school. The concerns of school staff are often conveyed during initial meetings with schools when the pitch is made to conduct research in that school. Listening to and following up on these concerns raised by stakeholders can assist scholars in identifying targets of opportunities for future research.

Produce Newsletter for Study Participants

We also share our findings with the families in our study by producing a short annual newsletter, *Safe Schools and Healthy Students*, that presents recent findings from our current data as well as general information relevant to the participants in our sample (e.g., information about the college application process for high school juniors). Producing annual newsletters has allowed us to forge positive connections with our study participants. Moreover, the general content of the newsletter has allowed us to give back to our participants, while the findings we present from the study data illustrate to participants the value of their participation. On a practical note, mailing the newsletters to students' home addresses also helps us to keep in contact with our participants across school years by providing a check of their current addresses. In choosing the content of the newsletter, we take care not to focus on issues that will single out a specific group of kids or raise concerns about the direction of the research.

Because the particular dissemination methods that will work best vary from school to school, school personnel are the best source for ideas about the topics of most interest to their students, teachers, and administrators and the best methods for reaching these audiences. To illustrate the value of school personnel to shaping the content and method of dissemination, Exhibit 9.1 contains strategies for more effective communication with stakeholders from a current school administrator.

Exhibit 9.1	
Strategies for Communicating With Stakeholders	
Know your audience	Target areas of interest/concern
Students Share information about the study by utilizing outlets that already exist, such as a school newspaper or magazine. Teachers Place a short newsletter in teachers' mailboxes as an effective way to share findings. Provide a list of resources such as books or Web sites where teachers can go for further information on the issues raised in the newsletter.	1. What can teachers and administrators do to enhance students' school success? 2. What are students' concerns? How can we be sure their voices are heard? 3. What can be done to facilitate family–school relationships?

(continued)

Exhibit 9.1	
Strategies for Communicating With Stakeholders (*Continued*)	
Know your audience	Target areas of interest/concern
Allow for two-way communication by providing opportunities for feedback from the teachers on the information you share with them. School administrators 　Communicate your research findings through electronic means (e.g., e-mail your newsletter or Web site address). 　Highlight how your research findings are relevant to them and their school. 　Establish credibility to increase trust in your scholarship.	

Note. These strategies were provided by Fernando Bibian, the Title 1 coordinator at Reseda High School in Reseda, California.

SUMMARY

In this chapter, we argued that scholars of developmental and educational processes should adopt broad dissemination as a goal, and we reviewed several options for communicating research findings. However, dissemination should not be viewed as the end goal. Rather, dissemination can be viewed as one way of facilitating the translation of scholarship into effective educational policy and practice. Increasing communication between scholars and the public can yield collaborations in which rich models of learning situated within particular individuals, schools, and communities can be developed and evaluated (Maton & Bishop-Josef, 2006; Sherrod, 1999). These types of collaborations can then form the basis for sound educational policy designed to improve the well-being of children and adolescents.

REFERENCES

Bellmore, A. D., Witkow, M. R., Graham, S., & Juvonen, J. (2004). Beyond the individual: The impact of ethnic context and classroom behavioral norms on victims' adjustment. *Developmental Psychology, 40,* 1159–1172.

Coalition for Evidence-Based Policy. (2003, December). *Identifying and implementing educational practices supported by rigorous evidence: A user friendly guide.* Retrieved February 18, 2008, from http://www.ed.gov/rschstat/research/pubs/rigorousevid/index.html

Fisher, C. B. (1993). Joining science and application: Ethical challenges for researchers and practitioners. *Professional Psychology: Research and Practice, 24,* 378–381.

Groark, C., & McCall, R. B. (2005). Integrating developmental scholarship into practice and policy. In M. J. Bornstein & M. A. Lamb (Eds.), *Developmental science: An advanced textbook* (5th ed., pp. 557–601). Mahwah, NJ: Erlbaum.

Higgins-D'Allessandro, A., & Jankowski, K. R. B. (2002). *Science for society: Informing policy and practice through research in developmental psychology.* San Francisco: Jossey-Bass.

Mahoney, J. L., & Zigler, E. F. (2006). Translating science to policy under the No Child Left Behind Act of 2001: Lessons from the national evaluation of the 21st-century community learning centers. *Journal of Applied Developmental Psychology, 27,* 282–294.

Maton, K. I., & Bishop-Josef, S. J., (2006). Psychological research, practice, and social policy: Potential pathways of influence. *Professional Psychology: Research and Practice, 37,* 140–145.

McCabe, M. (2005, October). Dissemination of science and the science of dissemination. *SRCD Developments, Newsletter of the Society for Research in Child Development, 48,* 2.

McCall, R. B. (1996). The concept and practice of education, research, and public service in university psychology departments. *American Psychologist, 51,* 379–388.

McCall, R. B., & Groark, C. (2000). The future of applied child development research. *Child Development, 71,* 197–204.

Rothbaum, F., Martland, N., & Bishop-Josef, S. J. (2007). Using the Web to disseminate research and affect public policy. In L. J. Aber, S. J. Bishop-Josef, S. M. Jones, K. T. McLearn, & D. A. Phillips (Eds.), *Child development and social policy: Knowledge for action* (pp. 265–280). Washington, DC: American Psychological Association.

Sherrod, L. (1999). Giving child development knowledge away: Using university–community partnerships to disseminate research on children, youth, and families. *Applied Developmental Science, 3,* 228–234.

Shonkoff, J. P. (2000). Science, policy, and practice: Three cultures in search of a shared mission. *Child Development, 71,* 181–187.

Index

About the Editor

Lisa M. Dinella, PhD, is a research scientist who investigates the relations between gender identity, academic achievement, and career development. Her research program is housed at the Gender Development Laboratory at Monmouth University, where she studies the social and interpersonal factors that influence individuals' academic and career pursuits. In collaboration with colleagues at the University of Wisconsin and Washington and Lee University, she researches the factors that are linked to young adults' academic paths, with the intention of isolating variables that often lead to disparities between men's and women's levels of financial independence. Her research has led her to create partnerships with school stakeholders in settings ranging from preschools to universities.

Dr. Dinella's interest in psychology and gender studies started as an undergraduate at The College of New Jersey. Her training in conducting school-based empirical research began at the School of Family Dynamics at Arizona State University, where she received her master's and doctoral degrees in family science, with concentrations in marriage and family therapy and child development. Additionally, she was an American Psychological Association/Institute of Education Sciences Postdoctoral Education Research Training Fellow. It was in this position that she met the network of school-based research experts who contributed to this book.

Dr. Dinella is currently an assistant professor of psychology at Monmouth University, where she serves as principal investigator of the Gender Development Laboratory.